GUIDE TO THE
QUAKER PARROT

Second Edition

Mattie Sue Athan

With 95 photographs
Illustrations by Michele Earle-Bridges

BARRON'S

Dedication

To Kawanita, Soldier, and Mr. Herbie.

All inquiries should be addressed to:
Barron's Educational Series, Inc.
250 Wireless Boulevard
Hauppauge, New York 11788

ISBN-13: 978-0-7641-3668-9
ISBN-10: 0-7641-3668-2

Library of Congress Control Number: 2007936499

Printed in China
9 8 7 6

Containment Ethics

Protecting habitat is no easy matter. If a pet bird flies away, go after it. Please do not release non-native species into any locale.

About the Author

Mattie Sue Athan has studied Quaker parrot behavior since 1978. She is the foremost authority on the tracking and recovery of lost pet birds, the author of *Guide to a Well-Behaved Parrot*, *Guide to the Quaker Parrot*, and five other Barron's Educational Series books on the modification of companion parrot behavior.

Please note: *Poorly socialized or unhealthy Quaker parrots may be a danger to the well-being of humans in the household. Escaped companion Quakers could represent an environmental threat in some places. Outdoor release or unrestricted outdoor flight of Quaker parrots is absolutely condemned by the ethical Quaker owner. This book recommends that Quaker parrot wing feathers be carefully trimmed at least three times yearly.*

Photo Credits

Gerry Bucsis and Barbara Somerville: pages v (top and bottom), 2, 6, 30, 35, 37, 38, 49, 54, 57, 59, 60, 61 (bottom), 63 (top), 64, 65, 66, 68, 69, 70, 71, 72, 77, 95, 98, 99 (top), 100, 104 (top and bottom), 106, 107, 113, 115, and 117; Susan Green: pages vi, 7, 8, 9, 11, 12, 13, 14, 17, 19, 20, 21, 23, 24, 25, 28, 31, 33, 34, 41, 42, 43, 46, 47, 53, 55, 56, 58, 61 (top), 63 (bottom), 73, 74 (top), 75, 78, 84, 85, 86, 87, 88, 89, 90, 91, 92, 93, 96, 99 (bottom), 101, 103, and 108; Pets by Paulette: pages 44, 48, 74 (bottom), 80, 94, 110, and 112; Shutterstock: page 22.

Cover Photos

Susan Green: front cover; Shutterstock: inside front cover, back cover, and inside back cover.

Contents

Preface

A companion Quaker can be both adorable and fascinating, but a Quaker is not exactly a pet. Even the best socialized individual may have occasional "temper tantrums." This is a remnant of the birds' wild nature and a part of their charm. They can be seen as little feathered "dragons," and sometimes they must be allowed to "breathe a little fire."

A poorly accommodated Quaker can be a flying feathered disaster looking for a place to happen. The difference between dream bird and nightmare harpy is appropriate environment and socialization for life in the human living room. The techniques described here usually produce cooperative, interactive birds that are a joy to be with and well suited to living with children (presuming the children can also be trained).

In a world of increasing human population, the Quaker parrot is considered an unwelcome pest even in its native range. Our living rooms may be the only places in the world where the Quaker parrot is truly welcome. Let's work to ensure that these delightful little dragons can adjust to the physical and behavioral habitats in human homes, for who knows how long they will be tolerated outdoors.

Even the sweetest, most charming Quaker can be occasionally temperamental.

Chapter One
Bird of Paradox

The Plain Bird with the Colorful Personality

Once before I had come to evaluate an African grey who never quite fit into this particular human flock. Now I was here to see a yellow-naped Amazon, the new third bird in the home. But the family's first love—and favorite companion bird—was a common Quaker parrot.

"Why didn't anyone tell us that the Quaker was the perfect parrot?" they asked me more than once.

They'd heard such wonderful things about African greys and Amazons, and such terrible things about Quakers that they thought they were missing something. Their two large-bird experiences only reinforced how wonderful their Quaker was. He used words with association, frequently learned new things, stepped up for anybody (away from his cage), and, after a decade in the home, he was still finding new ways to amuse his human family.

I'd heard stories like this before: Quaker parrot owners may be disappointed with larger birds even though the larger birds were purchased because they were said to be "better" than Quakers. But, occasionally, I happen upon someone who's seen groups of Quakers, maybe imported or breeding birds, saying, "I don't like Quakers."

And I might hear someone who has known maybe two or three Quakers (and sometimes even someone who wouldn't recognize a Quaker) repeat those same words: "I don't like Quakers."

It doesn't even sound like that first family and those subsequent "somebodies" are talking about the same bird! There must be a tremendous difference between the nice and the not-so-nice Quakers, for few parrots inspire such vehement opinions.

An unsocialized Quaker can be difficult, but hand-fed baby Quakers don't come into this world unpleasant. Why then, do some of them end up that way? Nature has something to do with it, but poor patterning and a poorly planned environment are

Baby Quakers don't usually come with behavior "problems," but they can quickly improvise and learn unwanted behaviors.

often the culprits here. A Quaker doesn't have to be a little tyrant, for these birds are very predictable and respond dependably to common behavioral techniques.

In *Myiopsitta monachus,* the common monk or Quaker parrot, I see all the mimicking ability of the budgie, African grey, and yellow-naped Amazon in a sturdy, easily manageable size. Indeed, in some places, these little grey-cowled feathered monk(ey)s are called "the poor man's yellow nape." In terms of price, size, temperament, talking ability, and accessibility, hand-fed domestic monks are everything one could expect of a companion parrot.

My own Quaker—who receives minimal attention in this home of many pets—is an amazingly astute conversationalist. At nearly 20, Tza-tza still laughs at my jokes and is nice to most anybody when inter-acting anywhere except in or o
cage.

Description and Origin of Name

Quaker parrots are bright gr
with a grey cowl across the he
lighter grey cheeks, and scallop
markings on the upper chest. Som
have a wash of yellow ochre acros
the belly. Although resembling conures, Quakers are the lon
members of their genus. There are four subspecies: *M. m. monachus, M. m. calita, M. m. cotorra,* and *M. m. luchsi.* Native to South America, they have established feral populations on every other continent except Africa. Several color mutations have been developed in captivity, and are increasingly available. Monks have no human-observable physical gender characteristics.

Certainly, the name, "monk" is derived from this bird's drab colors and markings. The grey cowl and face and scalloped markings on the bird's chest are not unlike the plain and modest attire of the Society of Friends, religious humans also sometimes called "Quakers."

Coincidentally, babies exhibit a sort of "palsied" response when feeding and begging. This quaking differs from the gulping motions of other baby parrots and may also indicate the bird's role in the flock. Some Quaker parrots retain this behavior longer than others; some revert to it occasionally when they are courting, ill, or otherwise needy.

While the terms Quaker and monk are used interchangeably here, I don't usually call this bird a "parakeet." Many people use the term parakeet because of the bird's long tail, but I believe that this word can be easily misinterpreted to mean that the Quaker is tiny and docile. Nothing could be further from the truth. This chubby hookbill has all the spit and vinegar of its larger cousins. Because of its strong resemblance to the two other families of long-tailed New World parrots—conures and macaws—I prefer to call *Myiopsitta monachus* a parrot.

Personality Traits

Highly social and eager to please (ready to learn to run the show), domestic baby Quakers usually love to be cuddled. Some birds never learn to step up (see Step-up Practice, pages 17 and 18) because they may be picked up like a baseball (with the palm around the back).

Baby Quakers might favor kissing and sometimes can be trusted to share tender nibbles rather than painful nips. They must be allowed to kiss only a clean, closed mouth to protect them from hostile microbes in human saliva.

Their talking (and noisemaking) capacity is legend. Hand-fed domestic Quakers often rival African greys in their ability to acquire huge vocabularies. Most Quaker parrots also learn to talk more quickly than most African greys. Hand-fed domestics seldom develop the calls of their imported predecessors. Wild Quaker sounds can be so repugnant that interlopers flee just so they don't have to hear the noise. On the other hand, wild Quakers are sometimes tolerant, even accepting, of the presence of other species in their huge communal nests.

Companion Quakers are also quite African grey-like in their tendency to bond strongly to one person or location. We see few significant behavior problems in domestic Quakers with a diverse environment, including a large assortment of well-used, frequently rotated toys. If adequate behavioral and environmental controls are maintained to prevent the development of biting behaviors, domestic hand-fed Quakers can be outstanding companions. As several of my clients have discovered, these birds might even be "better" human companions than some of their larger, more-famous cousins!

The characteristic quake of the baby Quaker parrot is unmistakable.

Better Feathers, Better Flight

Production and placement of illustrations is one of the final steps in preparing a textbook for publication. In 1997, while finishing the first edition of this book, I needed an illustration showing the six outer flight feathers on a Quaker parrot wing trimmed. A miscommunication occurred, and the drawings Michele Earle-Bridges sent showed the outside four feathers in place and the next six flight feathers (nearer the body) trimmed. But there was something unexpected, too: little fins jutting out from the edges of some of the feathers.

"Why are the tips of the feathers shaped that way?" I asked.

Michele explained that the illustrations were made from life, that she had examined the long feathers on her Quaker parrot's fully intact wings, and had merely drawn what was there: triangular structures sticking out near the outer tips of flight feathers 2, 3, and 4, counting from the outside.

I'd never noticed this. Those flight feathers were kept trimmed on Tza-tza, my own Quaker, and the rush to press was too great to allow further investigation. Michele quickly redrew the illustration, and I didn't think about it again for six years.

In the spring of 2003, when examining Winston, an adoption bird headed for Illinois, I stumbled across the same surprise. This wing trim was unusual, indeed. All primary and secondary feathers except the outer four had been cut on both wings. It was a lousy trim, but the real shocker was on those outer four flight feathers. Obvious and distinct fins protruded from the lower edge of feathers number two, three, and four (counting from the outside), exactly as drawn and described by Michele in the illustrations years before!

Immediately, I went online to ask Cliff Patterson and several other longtime Quaker parrot breeders if their birds had these unusual structures.

"What structures?" they asked.

But as we all began examining our birds, we found that Quaker parrots do, indeed, have unusual feather features on their wings. These structures are readily visible

Emargination on Quaker parrot wing feathers.

in many photos in the first edition of this book.

I've since learned that ornithologists call this unusual feather shape "notching" or "emargination." These features facilitate slow flight, maneuverability, hovering, and backward flight, and Quaker parrots are not the only parrots with emargination. Rick Jordan reports emargination on the wing feathers of the male princess parrot. Dianalee Deter has observed it on Senegal parrots, and Brad Stanley photographed it on red-fronted macaws.

During the American Federation of Aviculture Convention in Dallas, 2006, Zoe Howland, President of the Quaker Parakeet Society (QPS) led out-of-town members and Dr. Donald Brightsmith on a Quaker watching "safari" at White Rock Lake. While they were disappointed to see no active Quakers at the St. Francis Substation nest site, Dr. Brightsmith found molted flight feathers on the ground and questioned the presence of emargination. QPS members were delighted to share what they knew about those notches with Dr. Brightsmith, who is now conducting a study of flight-feather shape in Quaker parrots at Texas A&M University.

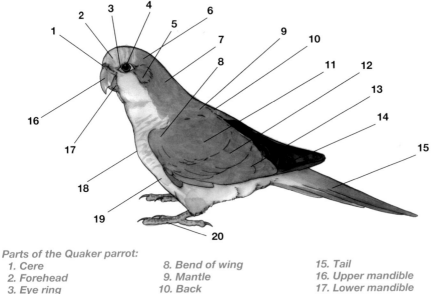

Parts of the Quaker parrot:
1. Cere
2. Forehead
3. Eye ring
4. Iris
5. Ear coverts
6. Back of head
7. Nape of neck
8. Bend of wing
9. Mantle
10. Back
11. Median wing coverts
12. Greater wing coverts
13. Secondaries
14. Primaries
15. Tail
16. Upper mandible
17. Lower mandible
18. Breast
19. Abdomen
20. Foot

Control and Other Issues

A smart little Quaker parrot might prove extremely innovative in trying to control *everything* in the social environment. For example, a companion Quaker might try to dominate the environment with its voice, a well-socialized Quaker would know to attack or chat with its toys, and a quiet companion Quaker might require more toys than other types of parrots. (Of course, almost anything can be considered a "toy.")

Unlike a "normal" (cavity-breeding) parrot obsessed with dismantling anything it can get its beak on, the Quaker often actually plays with its toys. A Quaker parrot might remove toys from the cage and will sometimes dismantle them, but this nest-building parrot may just destroy the components of the toy as many cavity-breeding parrots do. The bird may use the toys as tools, especially for personal pleasure, but an adult Quaker will be especially motivated to control *where* the toys are placed. More specifically, the Quaker wants to arrange things. Like a cat's interest in catnip, this develops as the bird matures.

The first home where I encountered a Quaker parrot was a three-person/three-parrot family. Mom had a baby blue-fronted Amazon, Dad had a shy, doting lilac-crowned Amazon, and the teenage daughter had an independent little Quaker that would go crazy when anyone touched its cage. The family didn't consider this a problem since the bird was absolutely darling away from the cage.

The cage contained a few dozen toys, including a little wire Chinese puzzle hanging from a chain. The girl would spend 15 to 20 seconds hooking the paper cliplike device to the cage bar. The bird would rush over to the misplaced toy (expending the famous Quaker curse), grab the puzzle, and, in less time than it took the girl to put the puzzle together, unhook it, administering a punishing "bop" before marching proudly away, fussing all the time.

If a plastic ladder was moved from one side of the cage to

another (there was barely room to move anything inside the crowded cage), the little bird rushed to pull and push and tug the ladder immediately back to its appointed place.

This need to control object placement in the immediate environment is more developed in the Quaker than in other, especially larger, parrots whose primary instincts involve removing objects from cavities. This drive to arrange things is probably related to the bird's unusual wild nesting habits. Quakers aren't usually compulsive "chain saws" like their cavity-breeding cousins. The instinct to arrange rather than destroy probably occurs because monks are nest-building parrots, a little quirk that makes several elements of behavior modification different for Quakers than for other parrots. It also makes the Quaker parrot an ideal choice for someone who has antiques and valuable fine art that might be quickly decimated by a cockatoo or macaw.

Hand-fed Quakers enjoy a well-deserved reputation as talkers that rivals African greys and yellow napes. Actually, a good-talking Quaker parrot may develop a larger vocabulary than either the African grey or yellow nape, but the words are seldom as understandable as those spoken by the two larger types of parrots.

Quaker parrots are a great dollar value for one who likes a little more spunk than a cockatiel without the issues accompanying many larger hookbills. They may be noisy in

Toy play is an important part of life for a companion Quaker.

multiples, especially if the flock includes wild-hatched or parent-raised birds. A single Quaker is an excellent pet for an adolescent, teen, or adult with limited space and resources. Actually, Quaker parrots probably achieve their best companion characteristics when kept as an only bird.

Behaviorally, I find the Quaker more predictable than brotegeris, conures, Amazons, cockatoos, or greys. They can be nippy in and around the cage, but are often docile away from the cage. Quaker parrots usually respond easily, quickly, and positively to the techniques described here.

Quaker Culture: Who Goes Where?

No other parrot lives and breeds in such close proximity to others of its own and other species as the wild Quaker parrot. This colony-breeding creature shares its constructed nests not only with many other Quakers, but also with other species such as bats, geese, and opossums.

While wild Quaker parrots allow these neighbors to literally walk across their "front porch," captive Quakers are famous for developing territorial-related aggression, allowing no one even near their cage. I call this "the Quaker paradox." How does an animal that is so tolerant of close side-by-side activity in the wild become so intolerant of others in its indoor territory?

First, let's look at who goes where in outdoor Quaker society. The three-room Quaker condo could be likened to an apartment (in a building of many apartments) with a bedroom, a living room, and a front porch. Different individual members of a Quaker's family are allowed to enter different levels of the Quaker's personal quarters. Mom, eggs, newly hatched babies, and possibly Dad are allowed in the bedroom. Older juvenile chicks and Dad are allowed in the living room. Neighbors, including, presumably, parents, grown offspring, cousins, in-laws, and other colony regulars can walk across the front porch.

How does the wild Quaker parrot know who has the right to be where in this complex social hierarchy? How does a Quaker recognize different individuals in the group? How does a Quaker recognize an intruder?

While some of this information is probably conveyed by language, I believe the first, most obvious way a Quaker can tell who's who in their society is by observing the individual's posture or body language. Baby Quakers have a signaling behavior that they are, indeed, babies—that is, quaking. A couple of years ago, I mentioned this behavior to a CompuServe correspondent who was expecting her first baby Quaker. She had hand-fed many baby conures, and when I mentioned quaking, she smiled—in computer language, that's :-)—and said, "Of course, all baby conures bob and gulp and beg when feeding."

I replied that Quakers are different. I heard nothing back for a few days.

On the third day, I received a long e-mail thank-you note. The lady graciously assured me that she would have presumed the bird ill if she had not been forewarned about the quaking behavior. "I never saw a bird do anything like that before!" she said.

I believe this quaking behavior in juvenile birds may be the way the parents know who is still allowed in the living room and who is to be pushed to the porch and outdoors. In like fashion, I believe the behavior of individuals in close proximity probably signals the residents how to respond to those individuals. If the neighbor is on its way home to feed its family and walks resolutely across the front porch—giving no eye contact, showing no fear—the resident adult Quaker will probably do no more than fuss or cuss briefly as the neighbor walks by. If, on the other hand, the neighbor is actually an interloper that makes eye contact, then quits eye contact, moves fast, shows fear, and/or retreats, the resident *knows* that the individual is *not* entitled to be there. The chase is on!

This interaction is probably the source of another important Quaker behavior. Especially in the vicinity of the cage, an adult Quaker might chase anything, regardless of size, that moves in the opposite direction. It's as though each little Quaker had the motto tattooed on its heart: "If you run, I'll chase you."

With appropriate training and supervision, a Quaker parrot can be an excellent companion for a confident, tolerant child, especially an only child.

Interactions with Humans

I believe that interactions with humans—especially humans who don't understand "Quaker society"—can reinforce the companion Quaker's natural instinct to chase any shy or unsure creature away from its territory. Some Quakers express this chasing behavior quite violently. Empathy, concern, and fear—all appropriate—fuel human behavior here. Repeating this interaction establishes chasing as a habit or pattern that is then frequently expressed and expanded. If an intruder has been identified and fails to retreat, there may be a loud and intense battle, and the intruder will be convinced to leave.

Chasing and Territorialism

Avoid the development of chasing and territorialism around the cage by training both the young parrot and all humans interacting with it in mutually supportive behaviors. If the bird's cage is 5 to 6 cubic feet

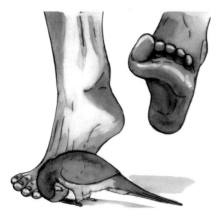

(1.5–1.8 cu m) or less, we might consider that the entire cage is the bird's "apartment." The "bedroom" might occupy the space where the bird sleeps and cuddles with the favorite cuddling toy, the "living room" might be the rest of the cage, and the front porch might be the top of the cage or the top of the cage door. With a larger cage, a flight, or walk-in cage only a portion of the cage might be the "apartment."

I believe that the primary human/Quaker relationship best resembles the relationship the bird would have with a flock mate, not a parent or mate.

One or two humans might expect to maintain a relationship of sufficient closeness with the companion Quaker parrot to be likened to a parent/child relationship. The parent of an adult bird might be welcome in the living room, but would probably never enter the adult bird's bedroom.

Most humans interacting with the companion Quaker can probably be compared to flockmates. Most humans are, therefore, best taught to expect the bird to step up peacefully and cooperatively from the "front porch." One or two favorite or primary humans might require the bird to step up from inside the cage (the "living room"), but the Quaker parrot benefits from being allowed to have a little private sanctuary where it sleeps or cuddles (the "bedroom").

Anyone trying to interact with a Quaker at the cage is probably the most influential factor in how the bird responds to that individual. Insecurity or fearfulness—especially if accompanied by retreating—can pattern the bird to chasing behavior that can become violent in the future.

In the interest of balanced relationships with multiple individuals, a companion Quaker is best frequently reinforced to step up from the front porch (the cage top or cage door) rather than from inside the living room, which might be reserved for only the most intimate friend. Step-up practice (see pages 17–18), including use of eye contact, the Wobble Distraction (see page 21), and Good Hand/Bad Hand (see page 24), is just as significant in the effective training of human handlers as it is in the effective training of the Quaker parrot. If everyone is trained to handle the bird with the same self-confident, sensitive, and predictable mannerisms, the bird's responses will usually remain cooperative and predictable with most, if not all, trained humans.

Chapter Two
The New Baby Quaker

Selecting and Purchasing a Premium Baby Quaker Parrot

Hand-feeding disasters can be devastating, especially to the bird; therefore, I believe that Quaker parrots are best professionally hand-fed and weaned. One might select a baby being hand-fed, then visit periodically to cuddle and begin socializing the bird before it comes home.

Karen Goodman, owner of the African Grey, a Colorado bird store, reports that in months when they are available (usually spring and fall), she sells more Quakers than cockatiels. "Because of their price and talking ability, Quakers are the best deal around. The domestic hand-feds are quite different from imports—less noisy, more talkative and cuddly."

Premium-quality hand-fed babies may be available seasonally and may be more readily available some years more than others. Ask dependable locals about when the best babies are available in your area. Often, baby birds are less expensive and there is a larger number of babies to choose from in the spring rather than around gift-giving season in the winter.

Quaker prices in the United States usually range from under $50 for older resale imports to over $200 for hand-fed baby domestics or in the thousands for new or rare color mutations.

Baby parrots should be professionally hand-fed and weaned.

BIRD ROOM RULES:

HANG ONTO YOUR
• CHILDREN AT ALL TIMES!

NO HANDS IN OR ON
• OUTSIDE OF CAGES!

DO NOT TOUCH ANYTHING
• WITHOUT DISINFECTING HANDS!

Know the Breeder

Look for a breeder or dealer with a reputation for healthy, well-adjusted birds and with a reputation for taking care of things if anything is amiss. Some breeders and dealers may offer little service after the sale; they may specialize in the "inexpensive" Quaker. Other long-term breeders or dealers may be known for servicing the sale—providing backup care information and other valuable help, such as, perhaps, free grooming, even years after the bird was sold.

Young Quaker parrots are easy to recognize. They have a soft beak, especially on the sides at the lower mandible, more green and less gray on the hood, and less pronounced barring on the breast. A young bird frequently pulls its head to the back of its neck and "quakes" when it wants attention.

Baby Quakers don't have fully developed immune systems. When shopping for a baby Quaker, be sure to visit only one breeder or dealer each day. Bathe, change clothing and shoes before visiting each facility. Many facilities will require you to wash your hands before handling their babies. Be sure to ask permission before touching baby birds, as some dealers allow babies to be handled only with supervision. This minimizes theft and protects the baby (and the interests of future owners) from mishaps involving mishandling at an early age.

The Noisy or Quiet Quaker Parrot

Many elements of the Quaker parrot's language are far from pleasant. If you wish a "quiet" bird, seek a baby that was not raised around noisy imported or breeding groups of

Quakers. This is tremendously important. Many Quaker breeders have a proven track record of consistently providing quiet, talkative Quakers, while some breeders don't have a clue about how to produce a Quaker parrot that isn't noisy. Be sure to research the expected characteristics of your new baby Quaker by talking with other people who know or own babies from the same source.

If acquiring human speech is important, ask the hand-feeder which babies are already talking, for many baby Quakers will acquire a few human words before they are weaned. Look for an active baby that is easily calmed with soothing words or for a calm baby that is easily excited by a new toy or flirtation. Look for a bright-eyed, alert bird that is interested in what you do. Look for a dealer who is willing to give a reasonable guarantee of the bird's health.

Gender

I consider gender to be irrelevant in the area of speech capability, but it may affect disposition. Now that sex can be safely and easily determined with DNA testing, many Quaker breeders and dealers have their babies sexed before selling them. This involves the removal of one drop of blood from a toenail, and sending it in a kit to a laboratory for analysis.* Many long-time breeders of Quaker parrots seem to

---

* Zoogen, Incorporated, United States 1-800-995-BIRD, Canada 1.519.837.BIRD, Europe/UK 44.0962.880376.

believe that the hens seem nippier. I can neither confirm nor deny these observations because I have known so many Quakers without knowing their genders, but I can confirm similar observations in budgies, lovebirds, ringnecks, and eclectus.

Territorialism

If the Quaker hen is the primary guardian of who comes and goes to the backroom of the family condo, that might translate into a more territorial hen. There is, however, great variation between one bird and another, and a male Quaker that has been patterned to chase and defend will be just as fierce as a female one. A female bird that has been appropriately patterned for cooperation will be as sweet as an appropriately

The first day in the new home is a common time for fly-away accidents.

13

An appropriate wing feather trim for a newly fledged juvenile Quaker.

I don't consider a Quaker parrot fully weaned until it can extract the heart of a tiny seed from its shell. Even if we don't intend to feed seed in the future, unless the bird can use the beak and tongue well enough to crack seed, I believe other chewing-related problems could develop in the future.

A parrot of any kind is a long-term commitment and should not be purchased on impulse. If you buy one while on vacation, be sure Quaker parrots are legal in your home state before taking it home. (See page 111.)

Bringing Baby Home

Before bringing the baby Quaker parrot home, be sure to ask the breeder or bird store staff to check to be sure that the bird's wing feathers are properly trimmed. The first day home is one of the most common days for an accident, when even a trimmed bird might fly or be blown away. Be sure that the baby bird has been trimmed in the manner suggested in this book (see pages 51 and 52). That is, all of the first ten feathers, the primary flight feathers, are trimmed to about a half an inch (1.3 cm) outside the covering layer of feathers.

Whether or not the new baby Quaker is trimmed in this manner, we should not assume that the bird can't fly until we get to know this

patterned male bird. The effects of territorialism in either male or female Quaker parrots must be mitigated with good behavioral practice and much handling and socialization out of sight of the cage. The primary area where humans interact with the companion Quaker is best out of sight of the cage.

Weaning

When purchasing a baby Quaker and waiting for it to wean, it's a good idea to visit the baby and handle it at least once weekly. Resist the temptation to ask that weaning be hurried along. Look for a dealer who lets each baby bird set his or her own pace for weaning.

particular bird better. Some birds can fly with very little wing feather, and a newly purchased baby bird has no business outdoors unless it's in the cage or carrier.

A mature companion Quaker can happily tolerate much cooler temperatures than most humans and many parrots, but when a baby Quaker endures the stress of changing homes, it's a good idea to keep it a little warmer than usual, maybe at least 78°F (26°C) for the first week or so. If it's cold outside, warm up the car before taking the newly weaned baby to the car. Put the bird in a rigid carrier that can be belted into the car for safety.

Most dealers will give a reasonable guarantee of the bird's health. As soon as possible, take the bird to an experienced avian veterinarian for a complete blood panel and any other tests that the veterinarian recommends. Although adult Quakers are sick infrequently, if illness is going to show up, it will show up in a baby.

Most states require that all parrot-type birds, especially Quaker parrots, have traceable identification in order to record and document change of ownership. This means that in most states where Quaker parrots may be kept legally, the baby bird will have a coded metal band around one leg. Usually, a domestically produced baby bird will have a continuous cuff-shaped band as opposed to the old-style split, donut-shaped bands that were applied to adult birds as they

A continuous cuff-shaped band may be applied when the bird is very young. A split band may be applied anytime.

passed through quarantine at the import stations.*

The band, however, can be dangerous to the bird. Be sure to ask the avian veterinarian whether or not the bird's band fits properly or should be removed. Since Quakers have a tendency to accidents, and broken legs resulting from caught bands are not unusual, many experienced avian veterinarians recommend removing a Quaker parrot band immediately. Be sure to record the band's number and/or letters and save the band with the bird's health and behavior history.

Visit an avian veterinarian as soon as possible to confirm the

---

* When a bird is DNA sexed, the owner may choose to have the DNA configuration filed with an international registry such as Zoogen, Incorporated, United States 1-800-995-BIRD, Canada 1.519.837.BIRD, Europe/UK 44.0962.880376.

An avian veterinarian should examine a "new" parrot of any age as soon as possible.

Try to bring the baby Quaker home as early as possible during the day so that the bird can get its bearings before dark. Provide the baby bird with a night-light, maybe one that plugs into an electrical outlet, especially if other pets might move around in the dark near the bird.

Watch the bird carefully to determine whether or not it's eating. It is not unusual for a newly weaned baby Quaker parrot to stop eating independently as a result of stress during a move. The bird may have to be returned to the hand-feeder for a few days for reweaning, or it might be stimulated to eat by watching another bird eat. Be sure to continue the bird on the same diet it was on before coming home.

Warm foods such as oatmeal and macaroni can feel like love to a newly weaned baby Quaker. Offer these warm, comfort foods daily for a while to enhance your bond with the bird as well as to guarantee a smooth transition to the new home. Eventually, the bird will probably refuse anything that seems like baby food.

Quaker parrots grow wise quickly. They are adept at manipulating humans. We probably have a window of opportunity of no more than a month to implement appropriate socialization practices before unwanted behaviors begin to appear. The ability to make the most of the baby days (see the following chapter) will determine whether or not this baby bird successfully adjusts to the home.

bird's physical condition. Expect the veterinarian to recommend laboratory tests. The costs of these tests are not usually part of the bird's health guarantee from the seller, but they could save expense and heartache down the road if the baby bird turns out to be harboring unseen illness.

If diagnostic tests determine that the bird has a health problem, a responsible dealer honoring a guarantee will provide treatment. Some dealers may expect the bird to be returned to them for treatment.

Carefully quarantine the new bird from contact with other birds until the veterinarian says interaction is safe. Most veterinarians will probably recommend a quarantine period of at least 30 days.

Chapter Three
Behavioral Development

The Baby Days: Patterning for Cooperation

When a new baby Quaker parrot enters the home, it is often still quaking in the manner of a neonatal bird. This provides a window of opportunity to easily reinforce acceptable behavior and pattern the baby to an emotional baseline with the use of step-up practice.

Step-up Practice

If everyone interacting with the bird practices step ups using exactly the same verbal prompt, hand positions, prompt location, and eye contact; and if the bird's responses have been appropriately reinforced, the bird should respond dependably to this interaction with any person. This is a matter of people training, for allowing untrained humans to handle the bird in unfriendly, or provocative ways can teach the bird to bite.

With the palm elevated, forearm perpendicular to the floor in a gesture similar to feeling for rain, fold your thumb into your palm and rotate your little finger toward your face, keeping fingers together until fingertips point toward the top of the wall to the left. Your palm now faces up with the little finger toward your chin. Place the baby Quaker on top of the top (index) finger. If the palm side of the finger tips is the highest point on the hand, the bird's instinct to climb will keep it on the palm rather than the wrist or forearm.

Successful practice stepping up establishes and maintains cooperation as part of the human/bird interaction.

Once the bird has one foot on the front hand, hold that hand steady, and lower the back hand. The bird will naturally prefer the higher stationary hand rather than the moving lower hand.

Since eye contact is an important part of this process, the bird must face you. If the bird is facing away from you while sitting on your hand, merely touching its tail with the other hand can stimulate it to turn around and face you.

With the index finger of the opposite hand (held in a mirror image of the hand the bird is on), gently touch the bird's thighs just above the feet,

If the hand being presented can be reached more easily with the beak than with the feet, then the hand may be bit.

maintain eye contact with the bird, and say *Step up!* clearly and distinctly. The bird should clutch one foot to the finger, then step up. This method of behavioral practice involves a verbal prompt (the command) and a physical prompt (introduction of an object to be stepped on in the same place every time).

At first it may be necessary to pry the little toes up to get that first foot on the front index finger. As you lower the back hand (the hand the bird was sitting on), the bird will complete the step up onto the front hand.

Practice this exercise in unfamiliar territory, out of sight of the cage, a couple of times daily for a minute or so each time. Stop after a successful completion of the command.

The Bite Zone

Be sure to approach the bird from below rather than in front of the feet. There is an area I call *the bite zone* that is about 1½ to 3 inches (3.8–7.6 cm) in front of the bird's feet. The bird cannot reach the hand with the feet, but can reach the hand with the beak. A sweet, well-socialized bird may gently reach out and pull the hand to the feet with the beak in order to reach the hand to step up with the foot. A poorly socialized bird might bite the hand in anger or frustration.

Presenting the hand in the bite zone, then pulling it away from the bird's beak when offered (for whatever reason), is a good way to teach and reinforce biting. Once the step-

How to Tell When Your Quaker Parrot is Going to Bite

A Quaker parrot intent on biting will usually give fair warning of the behavior to follow.

The bird will almost simultaneously

- look at that which it wishes to bite, an approaching hand for example, visualizing the intended object with both eyes.

- open the beak.
- spread its feet apart for better grip on the perch.
- lean toward or perhaps rush toward the intended object of the bite.

Any bite is best avoided, as repeated bites may become habitual behavior.

up command has been given, do not move the hand away from the bird, but, rather, move it toward the bird, even if encountering the beak. To move the hand away can seem to the bird like something running away. This activates a common Quaker behavior and the Quaker motto: "If you run, I'll chase you!"

If we don't usually back down or run away from the baby Quaker parrot, the bird will not be reinforced and, therefore, will not learn to regularly attack. Do not encourage or allow anyone to wave their fingers in the bird's face or provoke the bird by poking at it with inanimate objects.

Transporting the Bird

The first days are also the best time to train the bird to depend on humans for transportation from one bird-approved place to another (see Transportation, page 28). If the baby's wing feathers are kept meticulously trimmed, and if roaming is not reinforced at this time, the bird will be much easier to keep out of trouble when the instincts for independence begin to appear.

Overbonding

It is necessary at this time to work to ensure that the bird does not become overly bonded to one person to the exclusion of all others.

A Stimulating Environment for the Developmental Period

Sometime between 6 and 18 months, the normal Quaker begins showing signs of the strength of personality and independence necessary to be an adult parrot. Similar to human children in the "terrible twos," the bird will be increasingly exploratory and experimental. It might become noisy and nippy.

If a baby Quaker was well patterned to step ups and other cooperative activities during the baby days and was reinforced to play alone, the "terrible twos" may be almost unnoticed, but, if these behavioral controls are not in place, the changes may be swift and shocking. This period is a tremendously important part of the young Quaker parrot's behavioral development, for if the bird does not become independent, other, more troubling issues—including shyness—may develop. Shyness and fearfulness are unusual in Quaker parrots.

The favorite person must enlist the aid and support of other humans to help the bird remain open and accepting of relationships with several individuals.

During the first few days in the home, it is very easy to teach the baby bird to expect constant attention by holding it too much. If the little bird does not learn to play alone, it will be overly demanding of attention and may develop related behavior problems such as screaming, biting, and feather chewing. Spend plenty of time cuddling and loving the baby, but don't cuddle all day and all night! Try not to hold a baby Quaker much longer than you intend to hold it every day for the rest of its life. Be sure to reinforce playing independently, for this will be the key to *your* independence in the future.

In the wild these juvenile birds would be busily learning survival skills. They would be following their parents and flockmates around, mimicking their activities and learning many new behaviors. I believe that opportunities to mimic, opportunities to improvise, opportunities to make successful independent decisions, and an understanding of

The Wobble Distraction

During the developmental period it might become necessary to respond a little more directly to test nips occurring during step-up practice. First be sure that the hand is being offered properly (coming from below and just over the feet). Then, if the bird nips the hand being offered, gently wobble the fingers of *the hand the bird is sitting on* (not the hand being offered and nipped) then steady the hand.

The bird will have to stop the nip in order to retain balance. It will soon come to understand that nips during step ups cause "earthquakes." This correction must be done quickly, gently, and sensitively so that the bird is not overly affected either physically or emotionally. This technique works best on birds with full wings or minimally trimmed wing feathers and should not be used if the bird falls.

the mentor-based relationship with humans will lead a companion Quaker parrot successfully through this period. Mental challenge is the key to success here.

During this period the environment might look a little like an educational nursery school. A bird constantly stimulated by interesting and diverse opportunities in the environment is not improvising challenging humans.

During this time a young Quaker may test human patience and responses to the feel of the beak on flesh. The best way to deal with nipping during this phase is to ignore the bite and the bird rather than run the risk of accidental reinforcement with drama (emotional reaction). If we simply put a biting baby bird down, it soon learns that if it bites, it will be put down. The bird will prefer to be playing with humans, and will usually discontinue the behavior in order to be allowed to continue playing.

We might respond to persistent nipping by practicing the step-up command. If the bird is in the mood to play, and nips are rewarded with something that seems like work instead of play, then the bird will learn not to break the mood of playtime with nips. We might choose to follow step-up practice with putting the bird down and offering an interesting toy or two. This combines work with distraction and reward.

A well-socialized Quaker parrot may develop many varied cooperation skills in order to be held.

Here again, the best response to an experimental nip is no direct reaction (especially, no overreaction), but rather planned and precise response. If nipping behavior is unintentionally rewarded with screaming, anger, or other drama, the exciting nature of the interaction might be deemed *fun* to the bird; the nipping is, therefore, rewarded. It will remain a part of the bird's behavior and will increase.

The bird will also test the limits of accepted behavior by challenging humans in other ways. It is necessary to prevent screaming, roaming, chasing, and other unacceptable behaviors at this time so that they do not become permanent parts of the bird's personality.

Continuing Education During Adolescence

As the developmental period analogous to the terrible twos fades, the young Quaker may become so cooperative that we are tempted to discontinue step-up practice. This is not a good idea, even if the bird seems totally docile at this time.

Usually, however, since the Quaker parrot becomes sexually mature at a relatively early age, there is little separation between the developmental period and the appearance of sexually related behaviors that might be called adolescence. Unlike companion dogs and cats that are spayed and/or neutered for behavioral reasons, companion parrots are allowed the full influence of their sexual and reproductive urges. Techniques described here are intended to enhance favorable behaviors in companion Quakers and suppress or minimize most behaviors related to breeding.

Some Quakers will be easily kept tame; some will be difficult. Expect every bird to be a little different, with vast differences between successfully socialized birds and unsocialized birds. The more consistent we are in all interactions, the more predictable the bird will be.

As breeding age approaches, we see heightened exploration and physical and emotional experimentation. The bird might even change emotional and/or territorial loyalties, becoming aggressive around a newly selected territory or a new favorite human (mate substitute).

If a Quaker parrot has been allowed to overbond to one human in the past, at this time, the formerly favorite human might be neglected for a more easily dominated companion. We must be careful at this time to ensure that the bird is not excessively defensive of the territory around any human so that previous and predictable loyalties will not be abandoned. It might be necessary to take an "arrogant" young Quaker parrot out of its familiar territory for at least a few days each year in order to have the opportunity to easily reinforce interactions with unfamiliar humans. Vacations and indoor outings (visits to unfamiliar territory) are helpful at this time. Even a simple car ride with the bird in a carrier can make a difference in a Quaker parrot's disposition. Careful transporting in a carrier and meticulous wing feather trims go a long way to ensure safety on these outings.

Control Issues

At home the adolescent Quaker parrot may become increasingly concerned with control issues, especially immediate environmental control:

- The bird might start attacking tissues or people sneezing or blowing into tissues.
- An adolescent Quaker might also attack someone cleaning with quick motions with paper towels.
- An adolescent Quaker might suddenly decide it "loves" (or "hates")

a particular dog or cat or stuffed animal.

- The bird might move toys from one place to another and become increasingly agitated if anyone has the audacity to move any Quaker-owned objects or return them to their previous locations. Of course, this is that nest-building instinct beginning to assert itself.

A young bird that is allowed a great deal of liberty in the home might become overly vigilant or aggressive around a suddenly and mysteriously selected territory. The adolescent Quaker parrot will be seeking both companions and interlopers in its reflections so expect heightened reactions to mirrors, shiny objects, and small appliances—the bird might attack the vacuum cleaner or hair dryer. At this time the bird might fixate strongly on an inanimate object, using it either as an object of pleasure or an enemy to be attacked (see pages 24 and 25).

A Quaker parrot typically selects one or more toys to attack.

"Good Hand/Bad Hand"

The maturing parrot might begin to bite even a well-placed hand prompt for the step-up command. This might occur especially when the bird is being removed from a familiar perch, the inside, or top of the cage. Sometimes this behavior can be defeated with improved handling technique.

Maintain eye contact and offer the hand to be stepped on, approaching from below, as usual. Just as the prompt hand begins its approach to the bird, present an unfamiliar object in the bite zone (with one hand) and give the step-up command (with the other hand) followed by *Be a good bird*.

Carefully maintain eye contact when practicing any cooperation exercises.

In other words, if I want a bird to step up, and it is threatening to bite the hand I want it to step on, I pick up a small object (a spoon or a TV remote or a piece of junk mail), hold it about an inch below and in front of the bird's beak, give the step-up command, and suggest good behavior. Usually the surprised bird, responding to the familiar behavioral pattern, and knowing what *Good bird* means, responds also by being what it is expected to be—a good bird.

Eye contact is especially important; a bird will often maintain eye contact rather than bite. If the bird's eye is distracted by the introduced object, it will seek to regain eye contact immediately rather than take the time to bite after being distracted.

Even if the bird bites, that unfamiliar object will be bitten rather than the hand being offered for step ups. The distraction object must be neither too large (which might frighten the bird off the perch), too small (which might be ineffective), nor toxic (soap or a piece of lead or solder).

Imagined Enemies

There must be at least one enemy who can be regularly thwarted. To a very real extent, the bird must select or identify this enemy independently, and an adolescent Quaker *will do* this. Of course, it is very important for this enemy *to not be* a treasured human possession or a living creature, so several potential approved surrogate enemies must be provided. Safe, unbreakable toys or loud, safe bells are excellent candidates for this Quaker-selected enemy. If an adolescent companion Quaker has no opportunity to

release natural aggressive parrot energy against an approved surrogate enemy at this time, the bird is likely to begin to express that natural parrot energy against whatever or whoever is closest.

If the bird is enjoying attacking a toy, leave them both alone. There will continue to be times when the bird will solicit human attention. Those are the times when the adolescent Quaker can be successfully patterned to cooperate with the use of praise, rewards, and step-up practice. The more successful behavioral experiences we have at this time, the more the bird is patterned and reinforced to cooperate, and the more likely the bird is to cooperate when it becomes fully mature.

The Sexually Mature Companion Quaker

Aggression

There will come a time when threats might be accompanied by

aggression; a bite might actually break the skin. A sexually mature companion parrot is usually more difficult to handle than a strutting little adolescent whose challenges might be mere practice for the future. At this time, new programs, people, and changes might be met with strong resistance. If, however, the bird has been patterned to accept newness and change, it's behavior might be maintained merely by manipulating the environment.

If a Quaker parrot has not been appropriately patterned to cooperate until this time, attempts to socialize or resocialize may be met with great resistance from the bird. During this time it is not unusual for both predictable and unpredictable bites to occur, especially in the bird's perceived "territory." Usually there will be plenty of warning: hypervigilance, eye movement, wing or tail display, leaning toward what it wants to bite, or other body language that usually accompanies biting in this individual.

The best way to deal with aggression at this time is to give the bird space. That is not to say, reinforce

A Quaker might form a courtship or rivalry with any available reflection.

obnoxious behavior; never allow the Quaker parrot to chase or harass. Merely return the bird to the cage in the calmest possible way. A bird nipping during a step up might be wobbled a bit on the hand it is sitting on. A bird being prompted to step up might be distracted with a toy or other inanimate object when being given the prompt for step up. I call this distraction technique "good hand/bad hand" (see page 24).

Excessive Territoriality

Lowering the bird's usual relative height, combined with increasing access to rainfall and exercise, will help to minimize pent-up energy that might otherwise be expressed as aggression. A bird that suddenly becomes excessively territorial must have its territory manipulated either by moving the cage or radically redesigning its interior.

Quakers are especially prone to decide that a particular chrome appliance is either a mate or a rival, leading to many courtships with toasters and wars with hair dryers. A sexually mature Quaker might decide

that no one is allowed near the coffeepot. A bird that has fixated on a human-owned object must be denied access to that object. A bird attacking a human-owned object might be picked up using a hand-held perch, a towel, or "good hand/bad hand," and placed with the surrogate enemy toy. Again, we must encourage and reward a companion Quaker for expressing hostility against the approved enemy toy. Hostile energy will *be* expressed somehow; it is best expressed against something rather than someone.

Excessive Vocalization

Expect to see sexual behaviors of various types. If the bird is regurgitating or masturbating on humans (see pages 77 and 78), just put it down. These activities are neither to be rewarded nor discouraged, with this exception: If the bird has a problem with excessive vocalization, reinforcement or provision for occasional sexual behaviors can sometimes replace some unnecessary vocalizing if other distraction techniques and frequent drenching showers prove ineffective.

There will continue to be times when the bird seeks human interaction. As we will discuss in the next section, effective socialization tools such as maintenance of patterning for cooperation with step ups, transportation on the hand, and an ever-changing environment remain the most dependable ways to maintain companion behavior in a mature Quaker parrot.

Chapter Four
Socialization

The Behavioral Baseline

When establishing communication with another human, we know that we can successfully understand each other only if we speak the same language. Likewise, nonverbal communication must also be understood and interpreted by both parties to have the same meaning. Dog trainers establish communication with a well-socialized dog by using the *sit* command. The cues the dog receives to perform the behavior are usually both verbal and nonverbal. Similarly, practice of the step-up command establishes the lines of communication between bird and handler.

The effective handler says, *Step up* (a verbal prompt), and gives the bird something to step up on. Then:

- The well-patterned bird steps up.
- The bird is rewarded for performing the behavior.
- The bird knows what to expect.
- The handler knows what to expect.

This is an absolutely predictable interaction in which bird and handler communicate to one another that they understand each other's expectations.

The predictability of this interaction may perform an additional purpose as well. Step-up practice functions in the baby Quaker's behavioral environment by providing a moment of focus, a place to begin all other activities.

This exercise is, without question, the easiest way to reinforce a routinely cooperative relationship between humans and a tame-to-humans Quaker.

New owners of baby Quakers who practice step ups twice daily outside the bird's territory benefit in several ways:

- The comfort of the absolutely predictable interaction can provide the human and the bird with an emotional baseline that can calm almost any emotion from fear to ferocity.
- The redundant face-to-face activity establishes respect and trust between human and bird.
- The baby Quaker quickly learns to say *Step up!* when it wants to be picked up.
- The baby Quaker that is well patterned to step up in unfamiliar

Practice any routine— enjoyable interaction establishes and reinforces cooperation in the relationship.

territory is more easily patterned to cooperate at the cage.

Transportation

Some Quaker parrots have a developed ability to abuse humans in order to maintain control. Many also have a tremendous capacity to develop cooperation skills. Transportation dependence can be a powerful tool for developing and maintaining cooperation skills in a tame, interactive Quaker.

The concept is simple: The bird must have one or more interesting "foraging" area(s) in which to spend time. The more time the bird spends away from the cage, the less territorial behavior will be expressed at the cage. If the bird must rely on humans to provide transportation to

and from the cage and play areas, it will be patterned to cooperate in order to be allowed to enjoy foraging in all possible areas.

I like to let the Quaker come out of the cage to the top of the cage or door before offering the step-up prompt, and I usually have peaceful compliance. This is the most common time for a bite, but a bite can be easily avoided with good technique and meticulous eye contact during the process of the step up from the cage.

When walking with an unfamiliar or skittish bird on your hand, it may be helpful to cup the palm of your other hand over the bird's head and eyes to prevent it from jumping or falling if startled or excited. When arriving at the play area, position the bird so that the perch to be stepped on approaches the bird's thigh at approximately the same point used to prompt it to step up onto the hand. I use the same command—*Step up!*—to get the bird from hand to perch as from perch to hand.

Balancing Bonding

The Favorite Human

A Quaker parrot may tend to bond strongly to a single individual or territory. This bonding, in and of itself, is part of the bird's appeal, but consequences of the bonding can stimulate fierceness in the bird's personality. The intensity with which the pugnacious Quaker defends a bond can be formidable.

Commonly, a Quaker parrot will select a particular human to be its "one-and-only" mate substitute. This human may be treated to courting and kissing, and the bird might behave totally peacefully toward this person.

However, with the appearance of sexual behaviors—regurgitation, masturbation, and egg laying—and sometimes even before, aggression may be directed toward even the favorite human. This is not unusual in Quakers allowed to tolerate only one person and attack everyone else.

While being the favorite person of a tyrannical little Quaker might initially seem enjoyable, even amusing, related behaviors can continue to develop in unexpected and distressing ways. It is especially unkind to both the bird and other members of the household for a favorite person to laugh when a Quaker parrot bites others. The laughter of the favorite human is a tremendously powerful factor in the reinforcement of behavior in any parrot, but especially so with the Quaker.

Attacking the favorite human can come about as a result of either displaced aggression or the desire to dictate behavior. If an overbonded, poorly socialized little Quaker is sitting on a favorite human's shoulder and a hated rival enters the room, the bird might bite, or even actually attack, the favorite person if it cannot reach the rival. Like other parrots, the Quaker parrot obviously believes that, "If you're not near the one you want to bite, bite the one you're near." Displaced aggression expressed toward the favorite human is sometimes more violent than direct aggression expressed toward rivals.

A poorly socialized Quaker might get the notion that it can bully its favorite person into accommodating its slightest whim, for example, Mom/Dad might be bloodied for refusing to share the toast or newspaper. The more exclusive the bond, the more violent the behavior might be against others, and ultimately, against the favorite person.

Birds that have been previously overbonded to one person may switch loyalties, overbonding to a different person, and begin attacking the previous favorite. This can be distressing, especially if the for-

Any parrot that bonds strongly to another parrot might decide that it prefers to have nothing to do with people.

Reinforcing Quaker parrot behavior exclusively with the words "good," "good bird," kisses, petting, or other affection rewards is both simple and effective. However, this may be less than ideal if the bird is to interact with more than one person in the home. Affection rewards are best delivered by a favorite person while food rewards may be accepted from multiple "trainers." That's a definite "maybe" there, as the bird might drop food, throw it, or bite when food is offered by "disfavored" persons.

mer favorite had not been warned about this possibility.

These behaviors—all complications of the Quaker's instinct to passionately defend bonds—are defeated with practice of step-up exercises and transportation dependence performed by anyone other than the favorite person. The bird is patterned to interact peacefully with multiple individuals by being exposed to appropriate handling by multiple individuals.

Outings

The Quaker parrot's instincts to protect territory fiercely can be lessened by decreasing the amount of time spent in that territory and by allowing the bird to fulfill something resembling "exploration fantasies." As noted earlier, simulated vacations and indoor outings into unfamiliar territory are especially effective in reducing territorial aggression in the companion Quaker parrot; however, careful transportation and meticulous

wing feather trims must be maintained to ensure the Quaker parrot's safe return from these outings.

It is particularly beneficial for a Quaker parrot to take outings into unfamiliar territory with less-than-favorite humans. This behavior technique works by improving the bond between the parrot and that human. If the bird is out in public, perhaps at the office, the bank, or the mall, with only one familiar person, and if that person is handling the bird appropriately and compassionately, then he or she will usually become the favorite human in that scary place. This is an "emotional rescue."

This change of heart may be only temporary and may be lost upon returning home. Once again, behavior isn't linear; the improved behavior may come and go and will become habitual only if it is repeated. Commonly, the person who takes the time to include a Quaker parrot on outings will be treated very well, both out of the home territory and back in the home territory. That person may still be limited in terms of access and interaction at the Quaker's cage but will enjoy the bird's good disposition at all other locales, such as stationary and portable perches, etc.

If the Quaker parrot is well patterned to step up to a hand-held perch, even the less-than-favorite human should be able to remove the bird easily from the cage door or top with a hand-held perch. This gives no opportunity to accidentally pattern biting at the cage. The bird may be taken to another location outside its protected territory, where everyone can enjoy a full range of Quaker affection and cooperation behaviors.

Outings with the least favored person in the group are a tremendously powerful way to defeat over-bonding to one person. Outings are probably best taken by birds with trimmed wing feathers. Careful containment in a hard-sided carrier safely strapped into the car will help to ensure that the bird returns home safely. Prudent driving is a must, as avians may be fatally affected even by very minor traffic mishaps. One sensitive, heartbroken breeder I know lost a hand-feeding baby when it was run over after falling into the street as the stalled car was pushed from an intersection.

A little snuggling or extra affection can soften a parrot's attitude toward less-favored people.

The Rescue Scenario

In the fable of Androcles and the lion, a lion refuses to attack a slave who previously had removed a thorn from its paw. Likewise, a Quaker that is rescued from physical or emotional stress may learn to favor even a hated rival. Opportunities to "rescue" a companion Quaker may come at any time, but the most common and predictable opportunities include the groomer and the veterinarian.

The bird's favorite person puts the bird into its carrier, and the bird is transported to the groomer or veterinarian by the less-favored human. After the bird has been poked, prodded, filed, and trimmed, the less-favored human will, by comparison, seem much nicer than the awful groomer or veterinarian. A few cuddles, step-ups, "pretty birds" and "poor babies" can soften even the fiercest Quaker's attitude to a less-favored human.

If the bird is returned to the same behavioral environment as before, the behavior can regress and the pattern of trust will be lost. The behavioral effects of an outing must be reinforced by improved handling techniques by less-favored persons.

Change Is Good

Any type of parrot can become excessively concerned with control of its cage territory, but Quakers are exceptionally likely to do so. If a parrot's cage is left for years in the same location, if perches and toys are not occasionally rearranged, we risk the danger of the bird developing the assumption that it can *completely control* its environment. Resulting aggression should not be surprising.

Quaker parrots usually respond dependably to manipulation of environmental elements as a means of managing behavior. We can reduce aggression in and around the cage, by moving it at least a couple of times each year. This could mean merely reversing cage position with the areas to which the bird is transported for play (foraging) time.

Weekly introduction of new or rotated elements into the cage environment can greatly lessen the Quaker parrot's instinct for control. The more often the Quaker parrot's cage is rearranged, the less likely the bird is to exhibit either fear or aggression in and around the cage and the more likely the bird will remain tame.

The Quaker parrot's ability to tolerate change can be seen in the wild bird's ability to adjust to impermanence in nature when even long-established colony nests are sometimes destroyed in storms or other predictable disasters.

Nesting Quaker parrots are constantly assembling, disassembling, and reassembling their huge communal nests. It's not unusual for one family's babies to come tumbling out onto the ground if a neighbor steals just one wrong stick at the wrong time.* If a companion Quaker parrot is not provided with a variety of interesting, reasonable changes, we can usually see ill effects on its behavior by the time the bird is eight months old.

Some Quaker parrots are intolerant of human intervention in the arrangement of toys. We can mitigate this aggression by rearranging perches and toys frequently, and by rearranging them when the bird is out of sight of the cage.

Failure to rearrange and rotate environmental elements may have adverse effects on a Quaker parrot's behavioral development. A Quaker parrot that is conditioned to accept change at an early age is also less likely to develop fearful behaviors and inappropriate responses to stress, both conditions that can lead to feather destructive behavior as the bird matures.

---

* Ilse Goshorn, Quaker parrot breeder, interview, 1989.

Environmental Enrichment

The Quaker parrot's ancestors evolved a metabolism that was well equipped to cope with a life of wild independence. The companion Quaker's indoor environment is often missing important behavioral opportunities such as flying, foraging, assembling, and recovering from being wet that the bird would be experiencing in the wild. These activities enable the bird to express energy. When energy is unused, as when a wing feather-trimmed bird (read here "couch potato") sits always in a cage, that energy may be expressed as inappropriate behavior.

We must find ways for the companion bird to use the energy it would use during foraging in the wild. For Quaker parrots, that means teaching the bird, at an early age, to play alone; toys are the tools to achieve this end, but almost anything can be a toy. I was stunned when I returned home one day, to find that Tza-tza, my three-year-old Quaker, had let himself out of his cage and had spent his time removing tissues from a pop-up box and hauling them into his cage. Now, when I see a feather-chewing Quaker, I can't help but wonder what would happen if the owners merely gave the bird a fresh box of tissue to decimate every few days.

Since the Quaker parrot is a nest builder, many birds benefit from opportunities to gather and assemble nesting materials. Flexible twigs and coffee stirrers might be woven into elaborate ersatz nests, and a Quaker parrot that is building is not screaming or chasing.

In the wild the bird would be physically and intellectually stimulated by elements of the environment, especially those elements related to survival. A wild Quaker spends most of its time foraging for food. In captivity food is provided in a bowl.

Part of foraging involves flying. Obviously a wing feather-trimmed bird is not going to be doing that! In captivity, frequent drenching showers can replace flying as the primary means of using excess energy. The energy expressed by bathing and recovering from being wet can help to prevent some of those temper tantrums Quakers seem to have so often.

Another part of foraging involves decision-making processes. I believe all parrots have more stable emotions and more confident dispositions from having access to appropriate choices. For instance, I like to introduce more than one element, such as toys and/or perches, at a time. Since every toy and every perch provided is appropriate, no matter which one the bird chooses, the decision will be perceived by all to be successful and the bird will have a happy, potentially self-rewarding interaction with its environment. Even if the bird does not choose to play with a particular toy or to spend time on a particular perch, its presence provides the bird with opportunities to feel happy and confident as a result of making a successful choice between alternatives.

An Understanding of Time

Also missing from life outdoors is instant access to an understanding of what time of day it is. In nature certain things happen at the same time every day: The sun comes up, travels across the sky, goes down; shadows are long, then short, then disappear, then are long again. Certain creatures come and go at the same time every day: Nocturnal creatures go to sleep soon after sunrise; fireflies come out just before dark; everybody naps at midday.

In many living rooms, a bird might see few indications that time is passing. A companion parrot might see the progression of the sun across the sky, but probably, in most homes, may see only that

A Quaker parrot with no understanding of time might feel abandoned and over-preen or chew off feathers when humans go on vacation.

The pet sitter might give a companion Quaker one new (or rotated) toy for each day the owner is out of town.

there is light at the window sometimes and darkness at the window other times.

The intelligent companion Quaker develops confidence and independence from understanding time. This enables the prevention of abandonment-related behaviors, including screaming and feather picking.

Sometimes, something as simple as telling a bird, *I'll be right back!* before leaving the room can prevent attention-demanding vocalizations. If humans keep the promise to return quickly, a human-bonded companion Quaker will learn very quickly what these words mean. I know a conure that says, *I'll be right back* when it walks out of the room, and if a conure can say it with understanding, a Quaker can say it with understanding.

Time Markers

In order to teach the bird what constitutes a day, a "time marker" can be provided by arranging to have the television come on and go off at the same time every day.

Ideally, a mid-afternoon game show or children's program with lots of color and excitement will more likely hold a bird's interest. Even if the bird doesn't choose to watch the television program, it will notice the theme song, and know that it is mid-afternoon and that the "flock" will be home for dinner soon.

Humans have the opportunity to explain to the bird that some things happen *before* "TV Time" and some things happen *after* "TV Time." Every day when we leave, we say to the bird, *I'll be back after TV Time.*

When preparing to vacation away from a young Quaker parrot for the first time, we are more likely to come home to a bird with feathers and a happy disposition if we explain to the bird exactly how long we will be gone. (Actually, it's not unusual for a Quaker parrot to welcome a favorite human home from vacation with one punishing bite!)

To condition a Quaker parrot to tolerate a longer vacation, begin by explaining to the bird that *We'll be back after one TV Time. We'll be back after two TV Times; that means we'll be back in two days.*

Chris Davis, one of the first to work in the field of companion bird behavior modification, suggests that we count out the number of days we will be away from home by showing the number with fingers laid across the palm of the other hand.

Counting

It's good to teach a Quaker parrot to understand numbers by counting as we drop favored pieces of food into its bowl. I *know* that these birds can understand numbers but I'd love to hear that someone has *scientifically* demonstrated that their Quaker can count. We have learned from Dr. Irene Pepperberg's work with Alex, the African grey parrot, that an African grey can answer questions about shapes, colors, and numbers of familiar objects. I believe that Dr. Pepperberg's studies with Alex could be duplicated or at least approximated with Quaker parrots.

If the bird understands that *one TV Time* equals one day, then it will learn to understand what it means when we say that we will be back after *two TV Times.* If we gradually increase the number of days we are away, a bonded companion Quaker is much less likely to suffer adverse behavioral reactions than if we simply leave for a two- or three-week vacation without letting the bird know what to expect.

Establishing time markers in the environment is also helpful in conditioning a Quaker parrot to tolerate being "abandoned" during the day. That is, if the bird is accustomed to having an in-home companion all day, and that companion takes a job outside the home, the bird may develop adverse behavioral reactions. If TV Time is well established before radical schedule changes are made, the bird will not usually react negatively to changes; TV Time becomes a constant in an ever-changing world. The presence of constants like this helps the bird to tolerate those changes.

Cuckoo clocks or other instruments that sound the hour may also be beneficial. Don't introduce them immediately into the room with the bird, however, as such an instrument can sometimes seem like an intruder. Better to put it in the next room either permanently or temporarily.

It's not unusual to hear stories about a Quaker parrot's understanding of time or the passage of time. I often come across reports about Quaker parrots that seem to be able to either "read" clocks or have some other means of knowing what time it is. Quaker parrots often become quiet and withdrawn just before favored humans leave or enthusiastic and vocal minutes before they return.

Acquiring Human Speech

Just as a baby Quaker can be virtually *guaranteed* to be occasionally nippy, a baby Quaker that was

Companion Quaker Parrots in the United States Commonly Use These Words and Phrases with Association

- "Step-up" when stepping up or seeking to be picked up
- "Hi" or "hello" when people enter or the telephone rings
- "No" when they or someone or something else is about to do something unwanted
- "Gotta go to work" when adults dressed in work attire are leaving
- "Bye" when people leave the room
- "Com'ere" when the bird wants to be approached
- "Be quiet" or "cut it out" or "shut up" (or a similar phrase) when dogs bark or other birds scream
- "Peek-a-boo" when playing peeking games
- "Gimme" or "good stuff" or "yum" when favorite foods are being prepared, people are in the kitchen, when it's time to eat, or when soliciting food
- "Thank you" when treats or other reinforcement are given
- "Nite-nite" when it's time to go to sleep

This bird's loose feathers and coy expression say "come 'ere."

sensitively hand-fed and socialized by talking humans can be virtually *guaranteed* to talk. These gifted little mimics learn to say what they hear, so if hand-feeders talk to the baby birds, the baby birds learn to use the hand-feeders' words to attract attention in order to be fed.

Since most elements of the Quaker's language are learned, if you wish a quiet bird, seek a baby that was not raised around noisy imported or breeding groups of Quakers. If talking is important, ask the hand-feeder which babies are already talking, for many baby Quakers will acquire a few human words before they are weaned. In this respect a Quaker parrot probably provides more immediate gratification than an African grey. I believe a Quaker can develop just as many words as a grey parrot, but with less mimicking accuracy and understandability than the African grey.

It is unnecessary to drive the bird crazy with recordings or redundant sessions in the corner or in the dark, for a baby Quaker will learn to say what it hears spoken often and with

Easy access to toys ensures opportunity for self-reward.

enthusiasm. Talk to other humans and pets in the way you expect the Quaker to talk to you: *Hi! What cha doin'? Gimme a kiss* are easy places to start. It is almost impossible for the hand-fed baby Quaker, socialized in the manner suggested in this book, not to learn to say *Step up!* with some understanding of its meaning.

It is especially recommended that you talk to the bird while it is inside the cage. This is manipulation of barrier frustration: A Quaker parrot can be stimulated to talk to achieve its desire to get out of the cage. It's possible even to teach a Quaker parrot to use appropriate words to ask (or demand) to be let out.

Teaching phrases and groups of words that involve ritualized answers or responses are beneficial in generating other behaviors, even other talking behaviors, as demonstrated in the following story:

My own Quaker parrot, Tza-tza thinks that my coughing fits due to asthma, involve ritualized response.

Kiwi, the Quaker that Sets Things Straight

Kiwi, my little green Quaker, has an extensive vocabulary. The only problem was that he only spoke around family members. When company was over, he zipped his beak, only to make me look like a lying fool. But this behavior was about to be solved by accident one day by a friend of mine. She came over for a visit, and we were trying to coax Kiwi into saying, "I'm a cute little leprechaun," one of his favorite sayings.

My friend said it the wrong way. She said, "I'm a *pretty* little leprechaun."

All of a sudden, Kiwi perked up, cocked his head, and, eyeing her suspiciously, said, "I'm a cute little leprechaun!"

He just couldn't tolerate her ignorance!

Now all you have to do to get Mr. Tweezerbird to talk is to have company say things the wrong way.

Paulette Jacob
Covington, Louisiana

When I cough, he coughs along with me. When I stop coughing, he says, in the most precious voice you can imagine, *Are you OK?*

While Quaker parrots are well known for using words with an understanding of their meaning, they have a tendency to assign their own meanings to certain words. For example, Tza-tza has heard me scold my yellow-naped Amazon, Portia, many times for unwanted vocalizations at inappropriate times. Tza-tza thinks that the word *Portia!!!* spoken in a firm, scolding way means, *Be quiet, you noisy Amazon!*

So, whenever any of my Amazons scream—Saucey, Lolita, Bubbles, or Bock-Bock—Tza-tza says, *Portia!!!* meaning, *Be quiet, you noisy Amazon!*

The Power of Positive Reinforcement

Once, long ago, a tall, shy man brought his baby cockatiel to me for "taming." The bird was a precious, parent-raised cinnamon pearl hen. The owner was unsuccessfully trying to teach her to enjoy human touch. She would not step up or allow petting. Seeking to scratch the little bird's neck, the tall man would quietly, stiffly reach out to her, and she would threaten to bite him. It was a behavior that he couldn't ignore.

I said, "Talk to her the way you talk to your wife. Tell her that she's pretty, and that you love her, and want her to be happy."

The man gave me a strange look, then practiced whispering sweet words to the little bird, which seemed to "melt" in his hands, learning in somewhat less than half an hour not only to step up, but also to allow petting.

A few weeks later, bird and owner returned for a grooming lesson. The little cockatiel was sweet, tame, and affectionate. When I commented on the changes—the well-reinforced step-up response, etc.—the happy cockatiel owner grinned and said, "If you think that's something, you should see the change in my wife!"

This wise young man had learned that *verbal reinforcement* (praise) in anticipation of good behavior (cooperation) is one of the strongest tools available in the modification of any creature's behavior. He had applied this technique to socialize his cockatiel. He had also successfully applied this technique to improve a human relationship.

Accidental Reinforcement

While certain spouses and baby cockatiels obviously respond well to loving praise, even the wickedest, wildest Quaker can respond to conscientious application of positive reinforcement. Actually, it's quite common to accidentally reinforce behavior, especially in a creature that is looking for any kind of attention. A normal, creative Quaker parrot that is trained to anticipate rewards for good behavior also usually becomes more willing to seek new ways to generate rewards and will gradually abandon activities that are not occasionally reinforced.

Laughter is probably the most powerful reinforcement for a companion Quaker. Screaming or drama of any kind can also reinforce behavior; therefore, if a human

Harvesting Behavior

I have yet to see a description of wild Quaker parrot behavior that did not mention what can be identified as gathering or harvesting behavior. The Quaker parrot is often observed to take one or two bites from a whole fruit, then drop the fruit to the ground. This behavior, which is also reported in wild cockatoos, is said to turn perfectly reasonable farmers murderous.

Once, when I was studying a pair of naturalized wild Quakers in Denver, Colorado, I came to understand the purpose of this behavior. The birds were raiding a backyard corn patch every morning at 11 A.M. We could watch them easily from inside the house. The homeowners

felt very blessed to be visited by parrots in this unusual locale, and wished to protect the birds.

At traditional harvest time the birds were observed to drop much more corn on the ground than they could possibly eat. We were puzzled by this behavior, although, as I said before, it is often reported from the bird's native range. As the winter progressed, we could see the purpose and value of this practice, for no matter how cold it was or how much snow was on the ground, those two birds knew exactly where to find that corn. The homeowners reported that they once watched the birds dig through 5 inches (13 cm) of snow to reach the cache of corn.

receiving a painful bite overreacts—screams, jumps, runs, cusses—a Quaker parrot might continue or repeat the behavior for the "fun" of the interaction.

Quaker parrots have been observed returning again and again—even in the snow—to eat previously "harvested" bounty.

Verbal Reinforcement

Using verbal reinforcement may sound subtle, but results can be dazzling. The Quaker parrot is an extremely verbal animal. Verbal reinforcement is absolutely the easiest way for most people to perpetuate desirable behavior in any parrots. Praise as reinforcement is often used successfully, even though humans may be unaware that they are reinforcing behavior in this way.

Other Rewards

Although food is extremely important to some birds, some Quakers don't appear to be influenced by food rewards at all. Also, their ability to be easily reinforced by food rewards may be mitigated by their gathering behaviors. Some individuals might take reward after reward only to drop one after another on the ground. This is not usually agitation, distraction, or stress response as seen in some other parrots. Few of these Quaker parrots are demonstrating alienation; they may be exhibiting normal gathering behaviors, or, like cockatoos, many hand-fed Quakers might be simply so crazy about people that they would rather play or cuddle than eat whenever humans are near.

The Setup

The first step to molding a Quaker's behavior with verbal rewards is to teach the meaning of the words *Good bird.* Most Quaker parrots respond emotionally to melodious voices in soothing tones. Teaching a bird the meaning of *Good bird* usually comes naturally, as a cooing intonation of the word conveys the meaning quite effectively. The bird may stretch, puff out, and wag its tail in response to a successfully awarded verbal caress. When we can see that the bird knows what *Good bird* means, then the *Good bird* verbal reward can be used to reinforce any appropriate behavior. We can also reward the bird any time it is not engaging in inappropriate behavior. The words *Good bird* can even, under some circumstances, be used to suggest—and, therefore, to guide—good behavior in a bird that is misbehaving or about to misbehave.

Either food or affection rewards—or both—can effectively reinforce desirable behavior.

Be careful not to overdo verbal praise; too much adoration can seem like a courtship to a sex-starved little Quaker. If strutting, neck stretching, feather-flaring sexual displays are frequently reinforced, we might wind up with a beautiful little fire-breathing dragon that bites, chases, masturbates, and decorates the cage with regurgitated food.

Anticipation

In recent years, I've come to believe that it is usually undesirable to use negative terms such as *Bad bird,* especially when prompting the bird to step up. It can be confusing to hear both *Step-up* and *No* or *Don't bite* at the same time. If we want a Quaker parrot to do something, we must give only one message at a time. The words *Good bird* offer a clearer, more definitive way to both reinforce appropriate behavior and to prevent inappropriate behavior.

As with other parrots, positive reinforcement of appropriate behavior, not punishment for inappropriate behavior, is the most effective means of ensuring long-term cooperation from a Quaker parrot. Yelling *No*, *Don't*, or *Stop* will interrupt a behavior only momentarily. The bird may stop, look up, then go back to the previous (inappropriate) behavior.

Saying, *Be a good bird!* not only stops an inappropriate behavior; it suggests to the bird the appropriate behavior that should follow.

The bird learns that fulfilling the command, *Be a good bird!* brings surprisingly happy rewards. It reminds the bird that good things come to good birds. You will have stimulated appropriate behavior by reminding the bird of the rewards that go with them. You will have also reinforced a desirable pattern that is then more likely to remain habitual. It

may sometimes be necessary to combine this technique with a Wobble Distraction (see page 21).

Softly and sweetly reminding a Quaker parrot to *Be a good bird* is especially persuasive during practice of step-up exercises and when used in combination with "Good Hand/Bad Hand" (see page 24). This suggests to the bird what to do next—to be good and/or pretty. These words can often generate appropriate self-rewarding activities in a well-socialized Quaker parrot. The bird will discontinue what it is doing and initiate playing, talking, or preening behaviors.

When delivered sharply, firmly, and with authority, the words *Be a good bird!* can stop a well-socialized Quaker in its tracks. This might be used in combination with a hand clap or slapping a newspaper or magazine against the table if the bird is attacking or chasing and we are too far away to intervene physically. Again, we have both stopped the unwanted behavior and suggested appropriate—often self-rewarding—behavior to follow.

Maintaining Trust

Like other flocking avians, Quaker parrots commonly try to drive away both intruders and sick, thrifty, or less hardy birds so that predators won't be attracted to the flock. A particular human might be treated as territory, a possession, an intruder, or a rival.

A successful relationship between human and companion bird casts the human in the role of loving "teacher." Because parrots have a strong instinct to understand what is expected of them, two-way trust is probably the best way to maintain a long-term relationship between human and parrot. This may be easily accomplished with the frequent (most days) practice of the step-up, which patterns the bird to cooperate with other human expectations.

It is difficult to maintain a long-term, peaceful relationship with a Quaker parrot that is allowed to choose access to the human shoulder; this is doubly true for a poorly patterned bird. It is almost impossible to give a step-up command and maintain eye contact with a Quaker parrot on one's shoulder. Additionally, if the bird gets the notion that it has a right to the "dominant position" on a human shoulder, then that human might wind up being treated as territory or a possession. An angry Quaker parrot expressing overt or displaced aggression when sitting on a human shoulder can do painful damage to sensitive eye, ear, nose, and lip tissue, especially on children.

Extraneous body language—waving hands about and bobbing heads—can be very provocative to a nippy bird. Just as parrots that favor females may be responding to a particular style of reinforcement, parrots favoring males may be expressing an attraction to stolid body language and comfortable use of authority. The bird's behavior can

It can be difficult to maintain a long-term, peaceful relationship with a Quaker parrot allowed frequent access to the shoulder.

be changed by coaching the human client either to improve nurturing or effective guiding interactions.

Just one bird might respond to snuggling and praise, another might respond best to learning situations.

Potty Training

While a Quaker parrot's droppings are neither large nor foul smelling, many people prefer to train a companion bird to avoid soiling human clothing or furnishings with droppings. This can be accomplished by socializing the bird to void on an approved surface or location. The bird is thus patterned to defecate on the cage, perch, or a newspaper.

Potty training works exactly like any other kind of parrot training: We generate the desired behavior, then reinforce it until it becomes habitual. In this case, that doesn't usually take long.

A Quaker parrot will defecate to "lighten the load" just before flying.

To generate the behavior, we must understand it. A Quaker parrot probably defecates about every 20 to 40 minutes, more often if it's nervous. It will usually defecate every time it changes locations. For example, we can expect a bird to defecate every time we move it from cage to perch or perch to cage.

Humans can calculate the time between droppings, then anticipate the behavior by picking up the bird before it defecates. Place the bird in an appropriate location then reinforce when the behavior occurs.

It is particularly helpful to play with the bird during the first part of the cycle—just after defecation—then put the bird down to play alone for about ten minutes, before picking it up again to facilitate enactment and reinforcement of the behavior.

It's best to avoid training a Quaker parrot to potty on a verbal command. The Quaker parrot is a spontaneous and self-motivated creature. Although I cannot document a Quaker parrot dying from waiting for human command to defecate, I can document that tragedy in another New World species, the macaw. It's not worth risking a Quaker parrot's health for the fun of showing people that the bird will poop on command.

In some companion Quakers, because of their desire for human handling, potty-trained behavior appears spontaneously. If the bird figures out that it is put down when it poops on people, and if it wants to be held, it will discontinue pooping on people in order to continue to be held.

Chapter Five

General Care

The Cage

Size

A Quaker parrot that spends adequate time outside the cage in appropriate play areas can do very well in a modest-size cage. If the bird does little more than sleep in the cage, I think a Quaker parrot can be happy in as little as four cubic feet (1.3 cu m) of space in the roost cage.

I must emphasize that this is a *minimum* cage, and one that would be adequate if the bird slept in the cage and spent no more than three or four waking hours in there. This presupposes that the bird has frequent access to additional play areas (see the sections on Foraging Territory, pages 48 and 49, and Transportation, pages 28 and 29).

At the same time, an excessively large cage can contribute to behavior problems if the bird learns to avoid cooperating to come out of the cage. It is seldom difficult to entice a Quaker to leave a small cage—simply open the door. If the cage is small, the Quaker parrot is probably best patterned to step up off the door or cage top. In an appropriately sized training cage, if the bird chooses not

to come out, it can be easily convinced to "choose" to come out by removing the bottom grate and tray and turning the cage upside down, setting it on its top. The bird will readily step up off the "top" of the upside down cage, even if it will not usually step up willingly and peacefully from the actual top of the cage.

It can be quite difficult to convince a territorial Quaker parrot to leave a very large cage. If the cage is a flight or walk-in cage, the bird must be especially well patterned to step up to the human hand from inside the cage. If the bird is nippy, patterning to step up on a hand-held perch might be necessary in a flight or walk-in cage.

Although Quaker parrots usually chew a good deal less than cavity breeding parrots, they can easily gnaw their way through wooden or bamboo cages. Because of the Quaker parrot's suspected sensitivity to zinc, avoid cages made with any type of galvanized or zinc-soldered material. The safest metal finishes for a Quaker's cage appear to be powder coating, brass, or stainless steel.

Avoid cages with wide spacing between wires, lest a curious Quaker

A modest-size cage may be adequate for a bird that spends most of its time outside the cage.

get its head caught. Bars should be less than 1 inch (2.5 cm) apart. Quakers have less tendency to climb than many other types of parrots such as Amazons, so they can tolerate a glass enclosure so long as many interesting branches and climbing and playing opportunities are provided. I prefer a flat-topped cage for the play area provided by the top. Quaker parrots also tolerate a grate on the bottom of the cage, although many of them learn to pull paper and trash up through the grate for entertainment.

Perches

Be sure to provide perches that are small enough for Quaker parrot feet. Both hand-held and stationary perches should be furnished in a variety of easy-to-grip sizes. A bird cannot grip a perch unless the opposing toes extend at least a little more than halfway around the branch. Especially if the bird falls frequently, softwood branches such as ailanthus, sumac, or any of the poplar family are preferable to hardwood perches like manzanita, which is more suitable for full-sized macaws and cockatoos.

Covers

A fairly opaque—but not lightproof—cover will facilitate sleeping and noise control; a lightproof cover would neutralize the benefits of the night light we use to prevent injuries caused by darkness. A Quaker parrot sleeping in complete darkness might thrash about in fear and be hurt if it perceives movement in the room.

Temperature

A healthy Quaker parrot can tolerate much cooler temperatures than most humans. There is evidence to suggest that the Quaker parrot's immune system might be stronger as a result of some exposure to a cooler environment. A companion Quaker living indoors can easily tolerate temperatures down to 40°F (4.4°C), assuming no drafts.

Height

The height of the cage is significant in the development and prevention of aggression. A Quaker parrot housed higher than everyone in the house, especially children, might decide that it is the household "avenging angel" and will learn to punish everyone that comes into its territory.

Location

Even cage location is important. Place the Quaker parrot's cage well away from traffic areas where people move quickly. A person rushing past the Quaker's territory can stimulate the chasing behaviors and territorial aggression that are so well developed in the Quaker parrot.

It is especially important to place the cage well away from a doorway that people often rush through. If the bird is next to the doorway and doesn't hear someone coming, it can seem to the bird that that person appeared out of thin air, which can lead to all kinds of unfortunate behaviors from biting to feather destruction. If, in spite of the best possible choice of location in a particular room, the bird is startled whenever you rush through the door, let it know that you are coming by whistling or speaking before you appear.

Cleaning the Cage

Since Quaker parrots are not cavity breeders, they chew less, and, therefore, make a little less mess than other parrots, but they're still birds—and birds are messy. The easier a cage is to clean, the less likely that the bird will be homeless some day. Ease in cleaning may even be the most significant factor in whether or not the bird succeeds in its first home. The mess-catcher feature (horizontal extensions that catch debris before it reaches the floor) is optional with some cages. It is usually worth the extra cost.

I once heard Dr. Susan Clubb lecture on the suitability of various substrata (materials for the bottom of the cage and play perch). She reported

Hanging toys over a flat-topped cage can create additional play space.

that laboratory studies demonstrated that, in terms of disease prevention, newspaper with ink was superior to all other substances studied because it seems that ink retards the growth of bacteria and other dangerous microorganisms.

Dishes

If the cage comes with only two dishes, be sure to purchase at least one additional so that dry foods, wet foods, and water can be provided separately. Keeping bowls clean is easier if you have two complete sets for each cage. Just replace the dishes and run the other set through the dishwasher every day. A Quaker parrot is not the easiest creature in the world to live with. If cleaning the bird's cage is a difficult chore, humans may feel resentment, which can easily affect their relationship with the bird. Be easy on yourself and buy the most well-designed cage possible.

Foraging Territory

Separate play areas are necessary to prevent boredom, lessen territorial aggression at the cage, balance bonding, and facilitate cooperation skills. I like having at least one portable and one fixed, freestanding play area.

While tabletop play perches are inexpensive, easy to find, and often of appropriate size, a Quaker parrot on a portable perch can get into a great deal of trouble if it can easily hop off the perch to the coffee table or countertop. Roaming can be fatal. We can sometimes defeat this behavior by placing the portable perch on a backless bar stool. If the base of the portable perch is larger than the seat of the stool, then the wing feather-trimmed and appropriately socialized bird will be restricted to the perch.

I also like having at least one freestanding floor perch, preferably with a mess catcher. I love perches that look like giant Tinker Toys. I am, however, still just enough of a traditionalist to be very fond of freestanding softwood "trees." The weed trees—sumac and ailanthus—are excellent used in this way for Quaker parrots. Clean and disinfect branches with bleach water, being sure to rinse and dry thoroughly. Then mount chest-high forked ailanthus branches or whole sumac trees in Christmas tree stands, add toys and dishes, and watch the fun. If the first fork of the tree branches off at least 30 inches (76 cm) from the floor, the bird cannot get down easily. If the highest branch is no higher than the shortest family member's chin, the bird will be less likely to develop aggression on the perch. Some very short family members may be provided with a step stool, perhaps the type that has two steps and a handle.

Always keep appropriately sized hand-held perches nearby and pattern the bird to step ups on hand-held perches so that even the smallest or least favored family member can handle the bird when it is in a cranky mood. Behavior becomes habit by repetition. If the bird bites someone more than once, that behavior is easier to repeat and is in danger of becoming habitual. It is better to handle the bird with hand-held perches than give the bird the opportunity to develop a pattern of damaging human skin. A bird that damages human skin is also damaging human confidence, and this can do irreversible damage to the relationship between that human and that bird.

Toys and Playing

A Quaker parrot that does not learn to play alone is at risk of being neglected later in life. In other words, if the bird demands constant human attention, it is in danger of being physically and emotionally abandoned. A physically and emotionally abandoned bird is an abused bird; it will develop

A Quaker parrot is more likely to learn to use its feet to hold toys if it is encouraged to do so at an early age.

behavior problems as a response to that abuse.

Odd behavior can develop when the baby Quaker has too little to do: It might bite or scream because it has unused energy, or the bird might begin excessive grooming, such as preening feathers until they are damaged, chewing or filing nails, or sharpening the upper mandible on the cage or perch.

If we fill the bird's waking hours with step ups, outings, climbing, flapping, playing, and bathing, the bird is less likely to develop unwanted behaviors. Playing is especially important and usually comes naturally to the Quaker parrot, although each Quaker will learn different behaviors from its family flock. This animal is a parrot, which means it mimics—as best it can—the behavior of its companions. It's not unusual for humans in homes where a bird does not play to admit that humans in the home do not play either.

Play is self-rewarding behavior, and truly self-rewarding behavior

Look for safe toys from reputable companies that use guaranteed bird-safe fasteners and welded chain. While we have long known to avoid jingle bells (with the dangerous slits that can trap and cut little toes) and split rings (like those used for keys) for their dangerous potential, Dianalee Deter of Paradise Found, a Colorado bird store, reports that her Quaker recently found a new potentially dangerous item. Dianalee says that she had always been careful to provide only (presumably safe) quicklink-type fasteners for toys. One day she found her Quaker parrot hanging from the top of her cage with a small, open, quicklink penetrating the skin inside the cavity under her beak. Now Dianalee replaces all quicklinks for Quakers with larger, fatter quicklinks at least an inch-and-a-half (3.8 cm) long.

Another compelling report from one of the world's foremost avian veterinarians provides an entirely different reason for avoiding quicklinks altogether. Greg J. Harrison, DVM, co-author of *Avian Medicine, Principles and Application,* Ritchie, Harrison & Harrison, Wingers Publishing, Inc., Lake Worth, FL, 1994, suggests that zinc in the environment may contribute to feather chewing and self mutilation syndrome in Quaker parrots. He advises that quicklinks containing zinc should be avoided. Plastic self-locking cable ties can be used to replace potentially hazardous toy fasteners.

requires no outside reinforcement to be perpetuated. If the bird enjoys several interesting, self-rewarding behaviors, it will not usually develop behavior problems unless it is mishandled by poor socialization in interactions directly with human hands.

Playing can also be used to distract a bird from undesirable behavior such as screaming. If the bird can be induced to play with a toy rather than make obnoxious noises, then *the bird* can administer its own rewards, and the distracted behavior is easier to perpetuate.

A Quaker parrot won't destroy hardwood toys the way a cavity-breeding parrot would. Hard plastic and metal toys are relatively indestructible. A Quaker will remove the toys from the cage and will sometimes dismantle them, but won't turn them into toothpicks as a cockatoo will. Quaker parrots usually destroy rope and leather toys.

Be sure to monitor toy use, or the bird can't be held responsible for how it plays with toys. An amorous Quaker may improvise love games with toys. Of course, there will always be at least one "surrogate enemy," for our Quaker friends often have temper to express, and if that temper doesn't come out against a surrogate enemy, it will be expressed toward a human or other pet.

The creative Quaker can sometimes improvise unsafe behavior with "guaranteed safe" toys. Monitor a bird with a new toy to ensure that it has not created some dangerous way to use the new toy.

Trimming all ten of the long primary (outer) flight feathers on both wings will temporarily slow the efficient Quaker parrot flying machine. Expect wings to regrow at least twice yearly.

Necessary Grooming and Related Cautions

Trimming Wing Feathers

Failure to trim wing feathers can precipitate some of the most heart-wrenching tragedies a companion bird and its owner can physically and emotionally endure. From accidental escape to occasional disfigurements on the cooking stove, being closed in drawers, being sat on, or drowned in a toilet or tub, dangers posed by flight are real and potentially fatal. Having seen the results of worst-case scenarios, I am convinced of the necessity of careful, frequent, wing feather trims to inhibit flight in companion Quakers.

To ensure successful physical and behavioral development, it is probably best for a young Quaker parrot to learn to fly before wings are trimmed for the first time. Like many intelligent species, they may be suffer many falls if wings too soon or too severely be taken to ensure that not injured as they fly ind

Aside from the obvio of a flighted bird enco ceiling fan or being slam

p
su
extre
climate
dependa
sources of
food and
water are
available.

escaping through a door, a flighted Quaker parrot can incur "dispositional" damage if it learns to use that incredible capacity for flight to attack other individuals.

Complicating matters even further, not all wing feather trims will effectively ground a Quaker. Many times in my dozen-and-a-half years of recapture counseling I have heard: "His wings were professionally trimmed only a few days ago!" from a distressed human whose companion Quaker was sitting in a tree! Trimming either only one wing or allowing the end two or three primary flight feathers to remain long will *usually* fail to inhibit flight in a Quaker parrot if the bird catches the wind.

Even if a Quaker parrot's wing feathers are adequately trimmed to ensure that it will not become airborne, the agile Quaker can climb a tree in an instant. Quaker parrots should not be given liberty out of doors, whether or not their wing feathers are trimmed.

A healthy bird enjoying normal molts will probably require wing feather trimming at least three times yearly. Some owners simply maintain the trim by clipping each feather as it regrows. Of course, no feather is ever to be cut through the soft, flexible sheath that indicates blood supply to the developing shaft, but rather a new feather is cut only when it is completely open.

Grooming

Frequent owner maintenance of grooming can be part of intimate, face-to-face play between owner and bird. A Quaker parrot will expect a favorite person to groom its neck, a behavior called *allopreening* when it occurs between two birds. Since a molting Quaker may have a neck full of painfully stiff new feathers, a loving owner must gently break away the crusty sheath of the new feather. This is probably easier and works better when the feathers are wet.

Beaks and Nails

Quakers love playing hide-and-seek in the voluminous, soft folds of a bath towel or blanket. This is the Towel Game. (Variations of this game include Peek-a-Bird, Where's the Bird? and Where's Mom/Dad?)

While interacting directly with the bird during intimate towel games, we have opportunities to maintain the beak and toenails. Quaker parrots can have extremely sharp toe-

Quaker
parrots can
survive some
climes of
if
le

nails. Some Quaker parrots sharpen their toenails in their beaks or on abrasive surfaces; some Quakers blunt file their nails on anything handy. The way a bird maintains its toenails is probably a matter of personal preference possibly influenced by early experience with perches.

Sharp little parrot toenails can cause discomfort to some sensitive human skin, and if humans signal anxiety because of that discomfort, it can provoke the Quaker to attack. Well-groomed nails might be an important factor in maintaining a particular bird's tameness. Of course, be careful to nip off only the tiniest tip of a sharp toenail and always have a coagulant powder around to stop minor bleeding.

If a particular Quaker parrot demonstrates a desire to blunt file its own nails, that bird might enjoy a cement nail-grooming perch. While I do not advocate this type of perch for every Quaker, and, especially, I do not advocate installing it as the highest perch—the perch the bird would sleep on—I know that Tza-tza and other Quakers that blunt file their nails really enjoy this extra feature.

Likewise, if the bird enjoys sharpening the beak on the cage or accessories, and if the bird has a tendency to nip, a sharp upper mandible can break skin and negatively affect human interactions and confidence. Many Quaker parrots learn to love having the tip of the upper mandible sensitively filed by a favorite human with an emery board. Be sure to support the head on both

When trimming wing feathers, point the scissors away from the bird's body to avoid cutting a tiny toe.

sides with thumb and longest finger. Support the top of the head and upper mandible with the index finger. Be careful to avoid damaging the eyes. Be sure to use a nail file or emery board only, as a Dremel (power) tool can be too jarring for a small bird such as a Quaker parrot.

Playing the Towel Game occasionally, perhaps twice weekly, with the bird in the towel will maintain a happy, confident, and accepting attitude when the bird is toweled for physical examination. This conditioning to accept toweling could save the bird's life in the future if the bird is injured or ill and must be restrained for medical treatment (see page 59).

Hazards in the Home

Quaker parrots are probably much more likely to be lost to accidents than to illness. This can save lots of veterinarians' bills in a careful home or pile them up in a careless one. It places tremendous

A curious Quaker parrot can find an amazing variety of ways to get into trouble in a human home.

Oven Use and Cleaning

To minimize risk to a bird while you are using or cleaning the oven, it is best to have the bird situated as far away from the kitchen as possible and to ensure adequate ventilation around the oven (utilize exhaust fans, open windows, etc.). Even during normal oven use, fumes or smoke may contain tiny particles that, due to a bird's delicate respiratory system, can become trapped in the bird's lungs and cause respiratory distress (rapid or open mouth breathing, coughing, etc.). Regardless of oven type, when cleaning an oven, the bird should be removed from the area and adequate ventilation around the oven provided during the cleaning process. The manufacturer's directions should be followed for proper oven cleaning procedure. If oven cleaners are used, non-aerosol ones are least likely to harm a bird.

Margaret Gaut, D.V.M.

responsibility on humans to provide a Quaker-safe environment.

Next to flight-related accidents, being crushed is probably the leading cause of death in the companion Quaker parrot. These little characters really like to cuddle, and it's not unusual for a bird to snuggle under an Afghan or quilt that might be subsequently sat on with great force. Being squashed or suffocated is an especially common fate among Quaker parrots that are allowed to sleep with humans.

Because of their active and curious natures, Quaker parrots are vulnerable to being closed into closets and drawers. I once knew a lucky Quaker who survived for 24 hours in a closed drawer; it's a good thing that the bird's owner was meticulous about wearing fresh underwear every day, or the bird might not have been found in time!

Like all parrots, Quakers are fascinated by water and are often victims of drowning. Be sure to leave the toilet lid down if the bird has access to the bathroom. Be careful not to leave a half-full glass near the perch, for more than one hapless bird has been drowned headfirst in a glass carelessly left in reach. Unattended tubs, sinks, mop buckets, and dishwater have led to many Quaker parrot deaths.

Dianalee Deter reports that her Quaker parrots love to stick their heads into things: loops of string, too-large cage bars, and other unusual spaces. Sometimes, if the perch is too close to the food or water bowl, one of her Quakers will invariably find a way to get its head stuck. Be sure that any loops are eliminated from string, fabric, or leather toys. Rigid rings should be large enough that the bird's whole body can pass through. Replace all small clips, split rings, and quicklinks with self-locking cable ties pulled tight (see section on toys, pages 49–51).

While Quaker parrots are less prone to chewing than cavity-breeding parrots, they are still occasionally vulnerable to various types of chewing accidents. Exposure to lead, especially by ingestion, can be fatal. Common toxins in the home include:

• oven cleaners
• aerosols
• pesticides
• insecticides
• medications
• avocado
• chocolate
• alcohol
• coffee
• diffenbachia
• philodendron
• some other poisonous house plants.

Also, moldy foods are potentially toxic.

Quakers love to play with the same things humans play with, so they are usually interested in whatever is in the ashtray. Not only can a curious Quaker be burned by cigarettes left smoldering, but the bird can be poisoned by nicotine.

Misuse of polymer-coated and -impregnated cookware such as Teflon can kill all birds in the home within minutes. Fumes from other polymer-impregnated products such as stove parts, drip pans, coffeemakers, irons, and ironing board covers can also kill a Quaker parrot if the product is burned or overheated. If a coated skillet is overheated—over 500°F (260°C)—the fumes will poison the bird in minutes. I have often counseled in homes in which owners were well aware of the danger and owned *only one* such polymer-coated skillet, but not infrequently, this is the *exact pan* chosen by guests in the home.

All but one of the polymer fume deaths I have documented have involved inattention related to alcohol use. The story usually goes something like this: A houseguest comes

Loose loops in lace and crochet can snag tiny toenails and strangle an unsupervised Quaker parrot.

Any uncovered water is a drowning hazard.

home late after enjoying a few drinks, decides to fix tea or pasta, sits down, and falls asleep leaving the coated pan to burn. The pan catches fire; the birds scream to warn the humans just before they die.

Inattention caused by alcohol use can lead to a huge variety of bird accidents in the home. If you've been drinking, leave the cookware in the cabinet and the bird in the cage. If you do burn a polymer pan and the bird is still breathing, get it immediately into fresh air and rush it to the veterinarian before its respiratory system closes down. Something can be done if it's done quickly.

Because accidents can happen in the best-meaning households, I advise throwing *all* polymer-coated or -impregnated cookware away. It isn't worth the risk of losing a treasured bird because someone burned a pan.

Injuries from Thrashing

As with other parrots, a Quaker can easily injure itself thrashing in fear. This might occur as a result of a cage located where humans or other animals frequently rush past and seem to "appear out of nowhere," as when coming through a doorway or moving around in the dark. In this case, move the cage, call to the bird to warn that you are coming through, or notify the bird that you are with it in the darkness by talking or by turning on the light.

More commonly, however, Quaker parrots can injure themselves by thrashing as a response to loud noises, especially loud construction machinery, tools, backfiring automobiles, firearms, or fireworks. Fireworks are especially dangerous in stimulating enough fear to cause a Quaker parrot to thrash and injure itself. When it is likely that fireworks will be used near the home, try to keep windows and drapes in the bird's room closed and a television with sound on for the duration of the time when they might be frequent (such as on the Fourth of July). This will muffle the sounds of the exploding fireworks and lessen their impact, perhaps, by "tricking" the bird into thinking the sounds are coming from the television.

Medical Care

As mentioned previously, because of its robust constitution and inquisitive nature, a companion

Inherited Health Issues

Even some things that don't sound especially scary can wind up killing a Quaker parrot with a pre-existing condition such as a heart defect. I've known birds to succumb to heart attacks from loud noises—a slammed door, a dropped radio, a fly swatted with a book—grooming stress, or simply flying. These deaths aren't common, but they happen—especially in the Quaker parrot's smaller "cousin," the budgie.

As Quaker parrots develop more color mutations, they become less genetically diverse. Congenital ("birth") defects, such as a heart or liver anomaly, will probably occur with greater frequency. State-of-the-art medical care should be increasingly available to help us identify and treat these conditions.

Quaker parrot is probably more likely to suffer from accidents than from illness. For this reason you must develop a relationship with a reputable avian veterinarian, preferably by visiting the veterinarian immediately after the bird comes home. Additionally, you should know of a 24-hour veterinary hospital or clinic that is willing to treat untimely avian accidents.

Breaking Blood Feathers

One of the most common minor Quaker emergencies is breaking a wing or tail blood feather. As these feathers are molted out and replaced, they are covered with a white or bluish sheath indicating that this is an immature feather with a blood supply. If the feather is broken in the vascular portion of the developing feather, there could be a great deal of bleeding. Since the blood supply is rich in the developing feather, and very constricted at the point where the feather shaft enters the skin, the most effective way to stop the bleeding may be to pull the feather out. If bleeding from the blood feather is minimal and stops, don't pull the feather, but monitor to see that it is maturing properly, and pull it if it isn't.

A broken primary wing blood feather can seem pretty scary if the bird flaps and splatters blood on the wall. The first time your bird breaks a blood feather, take it immediately to an avian veterinarian or to the breeder or dealer who sold the bird. They can demonstrate

New color mutations may accompany other physical anomalies.

how to safely pull the feather so that you can do it in the future.

Restraining the Bird

To restrain a bird in a towel for grooming, to pull a blood feather, or for veterinary examination, begin by approaching from below rather than above as a predator would. First, confine the bird, then place it approximately in the middle of the towel, grasping it around the neck with one hand, joining the thumb and opposing finger (outside the towel)

Proper towel restraint for medical examination is more restrictive than the Towel Game, but doesn't restrict the expansion movement of the Quaker parrot's breast so the bird can breathe.

just under the lower mandible. Even if there is a little space in the circle formed by the fingers, if the fingers are directly beneath the lower mandible, the bird is restrained and cannot bite. Hold the other end of the bird—including the feet—with the other hand, being careful not to restrain the in-and-out action of the breast. Since a bird has no diaphragm, its chest must be able to expand, or it cannot breathe.

Once the bird is safely restrained in the towel, grasp the bleeding feather at the base with needle-nose pliers or a hemostat and pull it straight out in the direction it grows. An immature feather should come out easily. Then apply a small amount of coagulant powder. The bleeding will stop, and the bird will recover quickly.

Stress reactions to being restrained for emergency treatment can be prevented by desensitizing the bird to towels. A Quaker parrot that is socialized with the Towel Game (see page 53) to accept and enjoy handling in a towel will not usually experience an adverse stress reaction to being restrained in a towel when necessary. The Quaker parrot that is frequently toweled for grooming is also typically less likely to respond negatively to toweling during veterinary examination and treatment.

Band-related Accidents

Broken legs and other band-related accidents are also not unusual. Many experienced Quaker veterinarians will suggest removing a band, especially a loose band, to prevent a heartbreaking accident. Save the band, record the number, and keep both with your bird's records in the event you are ever required to document ownership.

The Carrier

Because of the danger of fire and the Quaker parrot's tendency to accidents, always keep the carrier near the bird's living space. If the carrier is buried somewhere in the back of a basement or attic, there will be difficulty reaching the carrier as well as emotional resistance by humans to getting help for an injured bird. Dr. Margaret Gaut, a Williamsville, Illinois, veterinarian, suggests practicing fire drills to see if all gear is ready and available quickly. When taking the bird to the veterinarian, Dr. Gaut says, "It is best to take the entire cage, if possible, without having to clean or remove anything from it."

Examinations

Provide annual or biannual veterinary examinations, whichever your veterinarian recommends for your

A safe band is neither tight nor loose.

particular bird. Quaker parrots are notorious for hiding illness—including sometimes-fatal egg-laying situations—until they are practically dead. If the bird loses weight, becomes listless, stops vocalizing, stops eating, or develops loose, runny droppings, get it to the veterinarian as quickly as possible. Keep an injured or sick Quaker parrot warm and quiet until you get to the veterinarian. If a bird is in obvious discomfort, give it Pedialyte or lactated ringers instead of water.

Diet and Behavior

Never underestimate the behavioral influences of diet. Timing and content of diet may be the most influential factors in the prevention and modification of all behavior problems. Examine and enrich a misbehaving Quaker's diet; a bird on a boring, inadequate, or erratic

When and how food is offered may be just as important as what is provided.

same bird can get to it in the future, it will "graze" on the food gathered earlier. This can be unhealthy behavior in captivity where the bird spends time in one place, soiling anything underneath with droppings. If a bird is handed one piece of food at a time at dinnertime, the perch must be cleaned before it spends time there again, or it could get sick from an accumulation of soiled food. Share meals with a companion Quaker by giving limited quantities of food placed in the bowl at the same time humans are served.

Feather condition, including the way the bird maintains its feathers, can also be an indicator of the quality of the diet. Broken, dull, or chewed feathers might easily signal the need for an improved diet, for the key to good feather condition is building strong feathers with balanced nutrition. This is usually easy to accomplish in a normal, healthy Quaker parrot with any of the quality commercial diets available today, supplemented with fresh foods.

From years of watching feral Quakers in the United States, I have become convinced that Quaker parrots enjoy, perhaps even need, something resembling grit in the diet. Oyster shell calcium is eventually digested, but oyster shell with granite, readily available in bird supply stores, provides both additional calcium and a little grit.

diet probably thinks it has good reason to complain or to be naughty.

Feeding on a schedule is especially beneficial in many ways, including prevention of unwanted vocalization. Provide balanced nutrition twice daily, morning and evening. Quakers also enjoy eating with humans, but, if they are fed by hand as they beg from the human table, we may see their "gathering" behavior.

A wild Quaker foraging in an abundant field will pick up one piece of food after another, take one or two bites, and drop the food. If the

Calcium

As with other parrots, Quaker parrots need a ready source of cal-

Never under-estimate the influence of diet on behavior.

cium in the cage, but other minerals are needed too. In the wild, dirt is probably a handy source for the many minerals needed to keep the Quaker parrot's body working properly. The need for multiple minerals may be the reason many Quakers demonstrate a preference for cuttlebone over calcium blocks. Cuttlebone is often a more diverse mineral source, as it can provide magnesium, iodine, and other minerals that might not be added to some calcium blocks. Dr. Greg Harrison suspects that Quaker parrots have a sensitivity to salt and suggests that they avoid high sources of salt such as human junk food, canned corn, fruit cocktail, grapes, mangoes, collard greens, carrots, and squash.*

Dr. Jerry LaBonde suggests a diet of "no more than 40 percent commercial diet"** combined with lots of fresh, unseasoned human food. My Quaker parrot, Tza-tza,

enjoys just a little low-fat Mozzarella cheese and some warm, good-quality whole grain toast every morning with his fresh fruits and vegetables.

Manufactured Diets

When providing a manufactured diet, consider mixing about 5 to 10 percent small seeds such as a canary-and-millet-based mix. Do not use seed mixes that include sun-

Beautiful feathers may be more than one meal, one month, or one molt away.

---

* Greg Harrison, DVM, telephone interview, 1997.
** Jerry LaBonde, DVM, interview, 1996.

Trapping a Wild Quaker

I had been repeatedly contacted by staff at a huge health maintenance facility that had been recently built in a landscaped and partially wooded alpine meadow. They reported that throughout the winter a small parrot would often huddle up beside the sheltered, sealed second-floor windows.

One particular nurse had continued to call about the bird every midday. My suspicions about what type of parrot was living wild in the Denver area were confirmed late one morning as I watched a large, hearty Quaker parrot eating mud alongside a stream through the snow-covered meadow. By feeding the bird and establishing a food dependency, the sympathetic support personnel had done half the job of capturing the lone creature. Placing my own Quaker parrot, Tza-Tza, on the Preview-Hendrix 125 cage/trap squarely in the center of a large patch of snow, I waited behind a shrub to pull the door closed behind the bird. It took only a few moments from the time she noticed Tza-tza until she flew to the cage, and only moments thereafter, she clamored into the cage for brunch.

The recaptured bird responded quickly to friendly handling and was adopted by a pediatrician in the facility.

flower or safflower for Quaker parrots. I see several advantages, behavioral and otherwise, to including at least a small variety of small seeds in the Quaker parrot's regular diet. Some Quaker parrots enjoy digging around in the food bowl and examining the size and shape of each morsel of food. They also enjoy the tactile pleasure of cracking seed. Accommodating these behaviors can help to prevent unwanted behaviors, including excessive vocalizations and feather chewing.

When using a good-quality manufactured diet, be sure to purchase the formula for companion birds. If you are feeding the manufactured diet designed to stimulate breeding behaviors, you will see escalating biting, screaming, and other behaviors associated with breeding. On the other hand, when rehabilitating a neglected bird, the enhanced nutrition provided by a breeding formula might be needed temporarily to overcome molting or health problems.

Vitamins

Resist the temptation to supplement vitamins without the supervision of an experienced avian veterinarian; in some situations, excess vitamins can kill a bird more quickly than too few vitamins. Be sure to not supplement vitamins if you know that the bird has a history of liver or kidney problems. The nutrients provided by real food—particularly when com-

A healthy, curious young Quaker parrot learns independent play easily when time alone with appealing toys is provided during the period between fledging and sexual maturity.

bined with a modern, scientifically formulated commercial diet—are more beneficial and less dangerous than supplementing vitamins.

Withholding Food

A Quaker parrot on a truly deficient diet might not have the energy or motivation to do much of anything. Withholding food is a particularly cruel and also inefficient way to modify Quaker parrot behavior. It is far more effective to distract the bird from unwanted behavior before it occurs.

Water

Of course, every parrot must have constant access to clean, fresh water. Many troubling physical as well as behavioral problems can be traced to no water, insufficient

Feather condition can be improved with diet and other environmental factors.

Hand-fed young Quaker parrots frequently learn human speech.

water, or dirty water in the bird's environment. Although Quaker parrots are known to quickly foul water in a dish, offering water in a dish or bowl is much preferred over a drinking tube. Most Quaker parrots bathe frequently when provided with a large enough container of water. Then, of course, the dirty bath water must be changed, but the presence of the water for bathing contributes to the prevention of attention-demanding behavior and self-mutilating behavior.

If, on the other hand, a particular Quaker parrot is obsessed with immediately dumping all the water out of its bowl every day, and there is fear that the bird's health might suffer from lack of water through the day, then a drinking tube must be provided. In this situation, the bowl of water is a "tool" for allowing the bird to continue its daily "watering" ritual (which may be a remnant of a healthy wild behavior).

Working for Food

In the wild, most parrots spend most of the day finding food and eating it. If they have to work for it, then the resulting behaviors are predictable and appropriate. For example, a Quaker parrot might benefit behaviorally from having to remove corn from a whole cob, perhaps with husks still intact. Provide occasional eggs and most fruits (preferably organically grown) unpeeled for maximum behavioral benefits.

Like playing, eating is truly self-rewarding behavior. To that end, many bird toys now provide opportunities to self-reward with found food.

Chapter Six

Occasional Problems and Their Control

Real and Threatened Aggression

Quaker parrots in the wild exhibit little actual territorial-related aggression toward known individuals of their own kind and they often allow storks, opossums, bats, or geese to share their large communal nests.* Paradoxically, companion Quakers are famous for developing and expressing aggression in their home territory. Whether defending a cage (physical territory) or a person (emotional territory), they are known to do so with intense determination. The following handling and environmental manipulations will augment patterning to the step-up command and transportation dependence to ensure a Quaker's good disposition.

- Control territorialism in the cage by frequently rearranging perches and toys.
- Control excessive bonding-related aggression by balancing bonding and not allowing the bird

to become emotionally fixated on one particular human or territory.
- Remove the bird from the cage to feed, water, clean, and add or rearrange accessories in the cage.
- Don't insist that a Quaker come out of the cage on the hand; allow the bird to climb out of that fiercely protected compartment onto the door or top of the cage where it will sweetly comply with the step-up command.
- Move the cage and play areas at least twice yearly; the more time the bird spends in one place, the more violently it may defend that space.
- Take the bird on frequent outings into unfamiliar indoor territory: the bank, the stairwell, the laundry room.

*Matthew M. Vriends, Ph.D., interview, 1992.

Only someone who knows this bird well can tell from its posture whether it wants to fly or is considering biting.

Safe indoor "outings" involving food and friends in unfamiliar territory are helpful in reinforcing cooperative bonds.

- Teach all humans expecting to handle the Quaker parrot to use appropriate techniques and procedures.
- Don't allow the bird to chase another living thing. Intervene if this happens, whether the bird is being provoked or is provoking another animal or human.
- Help the bird to express nervous energy by providing opportunities for exercise, including frequent drenching showers.
- Don't house the bird higher than anyone's head, and don't allow the bird to harass children and short people.
- Don't allow a poorly patterned Quaker parrot to sit on a human shoulder, especially a child's shoulder.

Excessive Vocalizations

The Quaker parrot has neither an extremely loud voice nor a reputation for excessive frequency of vocalization; however, it does have a well-deserved reputation for being able to learn to make some pretty obnoxious sounds. Therefore, reasonable residential soundproofing and/or understanding neighbors may be necessary in high-density living situations.

As with any parrot, a Quaker must vocalize regularly, but the raucous scream of the wild Quaker is learned behavior and does not usually appear in hand-fed birds raised by humans. It's easy to reinforce a Quaker in non-screaming behaviors, especially when humans are frequently present.

The Quaker parrot's natural tendency to learn human speech can be used to replace noisy behaviors. Redundant annoying sounds like "Ak (pause) Ak (pause) Ak" are more likely to develop in the Quaker parrot than actual screaming. I believe we often observe this behavior if food, fresh water, or favored humans are physically or emotionally absent. If the bird begins a pattern of repeating an annoying noise, we prompt it to say something or make a sound we do like, and reward the bird for replacing the annoying sound with the acceptable one. Ideally, we distract from this redundant "Ak" before it occurs on a given occasion, stimulating and reinforcing any inoffensive behavior. This might be a

What Do I Need a Secretary For? I Have Nicki!

Many of us champion socially responsible causes. While some folks concern themselves with Saving the Whales, or Feeding the Children, my own passion is the Demise of Telephone Solicitation. *I'm not interested in death-to-the solicitors, but to the invasive and inconsiderate interruption of my private time through the telemarketing trend in business.* I have a busy psychotherapy practice, and write articles and books in my "spare" time. Phone calls break my train of thought, but I must answer the ring as it may be a patient in crisis.

By contrast, Nicki, my Quaker parrot, really enjoys the telephone and often adds his two cents' worth to my conversations. My little green companion frequently joins me in the evenings, and his favorite perch is my left shoulder. That's precisely where he was last night, as I was working on an article for a parenting magazine about positive and negative reinforcement of behavior.

The phone rang. I placed it to my right ear and heard an unfamiliar sing-song voice say, "Good evening, and how are you tonight?"

My work was stalled, and my radar was on. "Are you trying to sell me something?" I asked.

Nicki's phone won't talk back.

"Oh, no!" came the voice on the other end of the line. "Because of your outstanding credit, Bank X has raised your credit line. Congratulations. We are offering you an opportunity to...."

As I was trying to think of the most effective means of negatively reinforcing this telemarketing behavior, Nicki spoke distinctly into the receiver from his vantage point on my shoulder. *Oh, Stop it! Stop it!*

Dead silence on the line; the caller hung up.

Clearly, the solicitor got the message.

Pat James Baxter, LPC, LMFT

---

nice time for a shower. A bird saying *Ak...ak* is trying to attract attention; most birds don't want to attract attention when they are busy resting, rezipping feathers, or are vulnerable because they are wet.

If a companion bird begins saying profanity or somehow comes up

Hand-fed babies raised in small groups well away from noisy wild-caught adults are less likely to develop loud vocalizations.

with an inappropriate word, try not to accidentally reinforce this unsuitable behavior. Laughter may be the primary facility by which this type of behavior is accidentally reinforced. The attention garnered when humans react with anger or scolding may also reinforce the behavior, so it is better to ignore the behavior until a plan for its replacement can be implemented.

One approach is to find a similar-sounding word or group of sounds that are just as much fun for the bird to say, then model and reinforce those appropriate sounds. For example, if a Quaker picked up the word *dammit* and we were offended by this particular word, we might quickly instruct associates and family members to frequently use and reinforce the words *can it* for the bird to copy. If the bird gets more attention for *can it* than *dammit,* the inappropriate word or phrase will soon be replaced (but not forgotten).

Quaker parrots don't usually vocalize loudly in the dark, so noise

control can be almost instantly accomplished by covering the cage. To prevent sunrise serenades, some Quaker owners cover their birds at night as a means of controlling when the bird perceives "daylight." Most Quakers seem to match the daily routine of the household and seldom begin normal morning calls long before human flockmates arise.

Toys Can Help

Toys, including bells, moving parts, and shredable rope, can be the first line of defense in preventing the development of boredom-related behavior disorders that include screaming and feather chewing. Play is a very desirable behavior. It is self-rewarding and easily learned by a bird that isn't reinforced to expect constant human handling and attention. Be sure the toys are small enough to be safe and easily enjoyed by a small bird.

Don't underestimate the allure of even very simple toys like paper towel or tissue bows (to be systematically removed) or coffee stirrers, straws, or twigs (to be arranged or woven into "nests"). Not only is a busy Quaker a happy Quaker; a busy Quaker is also not screaming.

When a Quaker Parrot Doesn't Talk

It's unusual for a well-socialized, hand-fed domestic Quaker parrot to not learn at least a dozen human words. These birds almost invariably learn to say *Step up*, *Nite, nite*, and almost anything else they hear frequently (see sidebar on page 67). I've even had reports of humans hearing escaped birds say *Step up* to attract attention to be recaptured. When a hand-fed domestic Quaker parrot doesn't talk, we usually find that the bird was housed only with birds that did not speak, was isolated from humans for the first couple of years, or (*very* rarely in Quakers) is expressing the consequence of ill health or depression.

We can usually defeat failure to talk in a young domestic Quaker with increased handling, improved modeling, and adding full-spectrum light and other environmental enrichments. Some birds may fail to talk because they are housed too low and don't wish to attract attention. Merely raising the bird and demonstrating the joys of increased attention will often produce words—maybe practice words—almost immediately. Of course, improved handling techniques may be required to offset increased aggression that comes as a result of raising the height at which the bird is housed.

Like other parrots, a Quaker will practice sounds it is learning at low volume. It's not unusual for humans to fail to recognize a talking Quaker parrot because they can't hear or understand them. In this case, we must improve modeling and rewards for improved understandability.

When a Quaker parrot stops talking it might be reverting to "bird talk"

A swing attached in only one place makes for more rowdy exercise than a swing attached in two places.

as bonds to humans lessen and bonds to birds increase. This might be a natural consequence of the introduction of another Quaker. It is one of the reasons I favor one-Quaker homes and feel that we will enjoy the best companion qualities in homes with *only one* Quaker parrot.

A Quaker parrot might stop talking because it is ill, injured, or experiencing stress related to the desire to breed. If a good-talking Quaker suddenly stops talking, it should be taken immediately for evaluation by an avian veterinarian.

A Quaker parrot might stop talking because it is depressed. Although this is very rare in Quaker parrots, depression can come about as a result of isolation, poor diet, loss of a favorite human, or loss of a

favored companion animal. Depression in a Quaker parrot might be related to something innocuous like a new light fixture or furniture that the bird doesn't like. Some birds are especially concerned about the introduction of lamps, noisy or invasive clocks, humidifiers, oscillating fans, or ceiling fans. This is a stress reaction and may be accompanied by other stress reactions such as feather destructive behavior. It is unusual, however, in a bird that has been conditioned to accept change.

We might temporarily move or remove the offending inanimate object, or we might try to desensitize the bird to the device by familiarizing it with the object. We might leave the fan in the room for a few days before we turn it on, we might leave a ceiling fan or light fixture on the floor for a while so that the bird gets used to its appearance, and we might use the bird's name in tandem with the object—"This is

Zeke's fan"—to further desensitize the bird.

A Quaker parrot might also discontinue talking as a result of the addition of a new pet or baby. Again, we work to desensitize the bird to the new family member, using their names in tandem: "Zeke's baby" or "Baby's Zeke." Leave puppy or baby toys and accessories around the house for a few weeks before the new arrival, and tell the Quaker parrot who (or what) is coming. After the new arrival, be sure to give the Quaker increased attention for a time and be watchful for opportunities to reinforce appropriate behavior. Temporarily raising the height of the bird's cage can help to offset this problem.

Molting

A couple of times yearly, but especially in the fall, a normal Quaker parrot will probably wind up with a neck full of something that looks like hard little spikes of carpenter's glue. These are pinfeathers or new feathers with blood supply. As each feather matures, the white covering hardens and flakes off as dander or feather dust.

Expect to see these new feathers soon after you notice that there are more feathers to be cleaned up off the floor and cage bottom. (Birds molt out of old feathers at about the same time dogs and cats shed.) The bird may be both nippier and noisier than usual. During this time, do

It's nice to have a friend to preen those new feathers coming in on the back of the neck.

whatever is necessary to avoid being bitten as redundant bites can become habitual. Indirect handling could be increased showers, more toys, increased vocal interaction, or eye games.

When the bird drops neck and body feathers, it will usually also drop wing and tail feathers. When we see the bases of those cut wing feathers lying on the floor, we know that they will soon be replaced by full, new wing feathers. Pick the feather up, and make an appointment with the groomer. The bird will have enough wing to fly within about a month, and, since Quakers are excellent flyers and famous "escape artists," their wing feather trims must be more frequently maintained than those of some other birds.

Feathers grow out with blood supply in a flexible white sheath. Wing and tail feathers in this condition can be easily broken. A broken wing or tail blood feather results in bleeding. If the feather is dripping blood, it must be pulled. (See the medical care section on pages 56–58 for instructions on how to pull a broken blood feather.) If the bleeding stops, don't pull it.

If the bird is kept in a temperature-controlled environment, some relief for incomplete or difficult molt might be found in sunny, warm afternoons outdoors or the addition of a little heat and full-spectrum light indoors. Retained feather sheaths on the head and neck can be softened with "rainfall," and sensitively removed by human or avian buddies.

Feather Problems

Feather destructive behavior is unusual in baby Quaker parrots, although a domestically bred baby Quaker, especially if it was parent

Irregular feather growth over the crop could indicate regrowth from incidental feather destructive behavior or might be the result of clumsiness in a recently weaned juvenile.

raised, might come with chewed feathers on the head. Since the bird can't reach its own head feathers, the presence of chewed feathers on the head is an indication that the bird was chewed by parents or companions.

But a Quaker parrot, even a baby, can develop feather chewing as a response to illness; therefore, any indication of feather chewing should first be evaluated by an experienced avian veterinarian. If the bird is causing damage to skin, we must consider that the behavior may be a result of physical illness. A Quaker parrot suffering from physically generated self-mutilation involving skin may require a collar or protective appliance to prevent self-injury. While these devices may prevent damage during physical recovery, they are of little benefit behaviorally and should be avoided when treating most behavioral feather destruction.

Quaker parrots occasionally develop feather problems beginning as a result of poor quality or old feathers, much of which is related to unsuccessful completion of the molt. Behavioral feather shredding can also arise, however, from any form of damaged feathers. A very snuggly bird might wind up with oil-damaged feathers from being petted too much with sweaty hands or lipstick-damaged feathers from being kissed too much. Behavioral feather shredding might result if the bird overpreens or tries to "even up" damaged feathers. This may be either a cause of or a response to stress.

The Influence of Diet

Feather-quality is directly related to diet. Be sure the bird has a diverse, interesting diet and that the diet is offered on a consistent schedule. Manipulate, usually increase, protein and calcium levels at least temporarily. Offer oyster shell calcium, grit, mineral blocks, and cuttlebone. Avoid giving a Quaker parrot salt of course.

A feather-shredding Quaker might be excessively active. If the bird is overly high-strung and/or underweight, we might manipulate the amount of hemp in the diet from 2 to 3 percent up to maybe 6 to 7 percent, or even eliminate hemp entirely. Evaluate the behavior of the bird after increasing or decreasing the hemp when considering further manipulations. We also increase opportunities for exercise, especially including rainfall (showers), as a means of expressing underutilized energy.

Lighting

Parrots need full-spectrum lighting to properly assimilate calcium. The duration of light during the day might be as significant as the quality of light. Consider increasing or reducing the duration of daylight to manipulate feather damage.

Abandonment

Behavioral feather chewing, shredding, or plucking can also appear as a response to perceived abandonment. As discussed in Chapter Four, we teach our companion Quakers a concept of time so that we can tell them when we are going away and reassure them that we will return.

Response to Human Stress

Behavioral feather damage can appear as a response to human stress in the home environment. Marriage, divorce, pregnancy, alcoholism, drug addiction, illness, depression—all can generate stress and stress reactions in the companion Quaker. These influences must be addressed to remove or neutralize the stress they create before we can expect improvement in the bird. Because Quaker feather chewing can escalate to self-mutilation syndrome, it's best to seek professional medical and behavioral assistance immediately.

Sexual Stress

Feather shredding or chewing may be related to sexual stress in

Feather destructive behavior is probably more common in Quaker parrots living with the stress of chronic pain or other physical challenges.

some cases, but it usually occurs in a mentally and physically under-stimulated bird. If the feather-shredding Quaker is insufficiently active and slow to complete the molt, I might consider offering a little extra thyroid nutrition and sources of vitamin A. I have seen excellent results from the addition of Ethical Nutrients Thyro Vital and Spirulina powdered and dusted on moist foods and combined with an enhanced environment and behavioral program. Again, we might manipulate the diet to increase metabolic activity levels. Enhance nutrition primarily with real foods, avoiding vitamin supplementation because of the danger of vitamin D_3 toxicity.

Manipulating the Environment

Success in training the bird away from feather shredding or chewing can be accomplished by manipulating the bird's environment. Any activities that stimulate the bird

physically can lead to the resolution of the problem. A bird that is hanging upside down bopping its toy is not overpreening and shredding feathers. A bird that is showered every day will not be chewing off

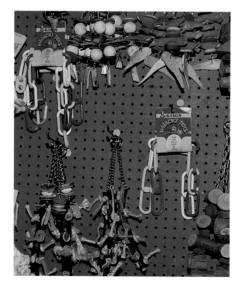

feathers when they are wet, and wet feathers are an opportunity to reinforce non-chewing behaviors.

Resist the urge to temporarily increase the temperature at which the bird is housed. The bird must not be subjected to hot, dry, direct forced air. Be sure the bird is housed well away from heating ducts. If we try to facilitate the molt by raising the temperature, we must also carefully monitor moisture and/or increase bathing.

Toys

Be sure to include multiple toys of different types so that the bird has the opportunity to choose which toys to play with. Just because a bird doesn't play with a particular toy doesn't mean it "doesn't like toys." It means that the bird isn't interested in that toy at that time. Unless it is afraid of the toy, the toy's presence provides an opportunity to exercise confidence-building, decision-making processes. As previously mentioned, avoid anything that may contain zinc.

Consider allowing the bird to have increased height, including possibly, enough wing feather to fly until the behavioral destruction can be resolved. As confidence increases, aggression, activity, and independence increase, and feather chewing declines. If a baby Quaker is housed too low, reprimanded too severely, or not allowed to develop at least a little "attitude," the loss of confidence could result in a sedentary bird. A Quaker with an understimulated metabolism overpreens, resulting in

Determination

After Maxine and Paco's first clutch of babies, I pulled their nest box to give them a rest. Maxine had proven to be an excellent mom, but because she was a "rescued" bird, I tend to spoil her a bit. Needless to say, she had different ideas.

When Max is upset, she "beats up" her favorite toy, her Polly-Dolly. Several days after the nest box came down, I noticed that the rope portion of her toy was on the bottom of the cage, along with a few molted feathers. Paco is building again, I thought. That same evening, the pair was doing their "cluck-dance" in the corner near the makeshift nest. Not again!

Two days later there it was—a new egg, carefully laid on the piece of shredded rope.

Janice A. Wagner
Charlotte, North Carolina

Quaker parrots don't usually damage wet feathers.

feathers with split ends that are eventually chewed off.

Eye Games

Manipulating eye contact as well as playing passive eye games can improve confidence in an anxious bird. Try playing Peek-a-Bird around the corner, the Blink-Back game, and "I can hold still longer than you can." Treat feather chewing in a shy bird by improving elements that build a sense of safety and confidence. As the bird's behavior normalizes look for more

nips and tail wags (perhaps keeping a record of the number of happiness behaviors observed each day). The feather chewing will stop and feathers will usually regrow.

A Quaker parrot that begins destroying feathers needs professional assistance immediately. Feather mutilation can be progressive and life threatening. Dr. Steven Feldman of Denver, Colorado, reports that he has seen a self-mutilating Quaker that came within a millimeter of severing its own jugular vein. He has also seen a Quaker parrot that *did* sever its jugular vein.

Allofeeding

As with other parrots, allofeeding (regurgitating) is one of the most common early sexual behaviors in Quakers. Even at a very young age, a happy, amorous Quaker may wish to provide the object of its affection with warm, gooey, partially digested food.

To a bird, this is romantic behavior—and Quaker parrots can be *very* romantic. To a bird being courted, this behavior says, "Look what a good parent and provider I could be! I could do a great job of feeding your babies!"

Humans may be less than excited by the deposit of something resembling warm oatmeal in their hand, hair, or ear. Obviously, this behavior must not be reinforced, lest the bird decide that the way to win friends and influence toys is by feeding them.

We occasionally see a bird with the vice of feeding everything, including perches, in the environment. This can be very messy.

With allofeeding as with other behaviors, distraction and reinforcement of the introduced behavior will redirect and replace the unwanted behavior. For example, when a bird starts feeding the owner's hand, simply say, "Be a good bird! Go play with your toys!" Put the bird down and ring its bell in its face until it gets interested in playing with or attacking the bell. We might hand the bird a tiny holding toy, maybe one of those little plastic barrels with a moving bell inside, then tell the bird it's a "good bird" or a "pretty bird" when it performs the distraction behavior.

Once again, laughter of the favorite person is probably the strongest rein-forcer of this type of behavior. If you laugh when Zeke feeds your hand or the telephone receiver, you might have to clean up a lot of goo during all the remaining days of your (or the Quaker parrot's) life.

Other Sexual Behaviors

Masturbation

The arrival of sexual behaviors might be signaled when either gender begins allofeeding a toy or other objects or begins rubbing against toys, cage, or perch, or their companion's hand, head, or other body parts seeking sexual fulfillment. Expect a male Quaker to form a consummated relationship with his bell. Some cocks pleasure themselves often, sometimes sounding more like a snake than a little green bird. Most male birds probably masturbate with the tail pointed down. Most hens probably do so with the tail pointed up or straight back, but there are many variables here, and tail position is not always an accurate indication of gender.

Just because a Quaker parrot masturbates doesn't necessarily mean that the bird is actually interested in breeding; it's not unusual for a Quaker parrot to prefer masturbation to copulation. Choice of mate may play a part in this, but probably, in most birds that prefer masturbation, this behavior is a matter of sexual preference that will not change

no matter how many attractive mate choices are offered.

Feather Shredding

Feather shredding appearing under the wings of a mature Quaker may be an indication of sexually induced stress (see page 73). Since the bird's sexual organs are under the wings, just behind the thighs, petting or other stimulation under the wings can activate breeding behaviors, including allofeeding, masturbation, egg laying, and sexually induced stress reactions such as feather chewing.

Egg Laying

A Quaker hen can begin laying eggs before the age of three. It is usually a rare occurrence in a companion Quaker with no sexual partner. Of course, humans may be petting the bird in a way that the bird finds sexually stimulating, and, while it is not especially unhealthy for a hen bird to lay an occasional egg, it can have adverse effects on her disposition.

Examine the amount of protein in the diet. Ideally, that level should probably be somewhere between 10 and 16 percent. Any time protein levels exceed 16 percent, we can expect to see an increase in all sexually related behaviors.

Excessive egg laying can deplete even the strongest constitution. A companion Quaker that is producing more than half a dozen eggs in a cycle should be seen by a veterinarian who can provide hormone therapy or perform a hysterectomy. If the bird has gone more than three days since the last egg, remove all the eggs so that she will not be tempted to develop the vice of eating her eggs.

Solutions

Of course, any sexually stimulating activities must be discontinued.

Baby Quaker parrots are altricial—virtually helpless for weeks after hatching.

The bird must be given projects and activities to distract from sexual behaviors. These can include increased showering and bathing, exercise, enriched environment, and better attention to speech training and patterning rituals. This might be a good time to give the bird a pop-up box of tissues to ravish or a whole box of coffee stirrers to haul and throw around. Be sure the bird has an appropriate surrogate enemy toy to beat up.

Both masturbation and egg laying can be treated with manipulation of light. The quality, quantity, and duration of light all can influence these behaviors. Especially consider manipulating the length of the artificial "daylight" periods the bird experiences.

A good-quality light source provides full-spectrum light. A hen, especially, requires full-spectrum light as part of the process of absorbing and utilizing calcium. This is particularly important for an egg layer. One hen might be laying because she is getting too much light for too long periods during the day, while another might be laying because she is getting too little light and has found a dark corner to crouch in—another activity that can stimulate sexual behaviors. Of course, manipulating the light would mean decreasing light for one bird and increasing it for the other bird. This is a trial-and-error situation; you may have to experiment to find the correct solution for a particular bird.

Retrieving a Lost Companion Quaker

Dr. Jerry LaBonde, who serves the largest avian veterinary practice in Colorado, has been heard to comment, "If it's flown away, it's probably a Quaker."

Indeed, in the vast Denver metropolitan area I have captured many, many free-flying Quakers, including one—of absolutely unknown ownership—only blocks from Dr. LaBonde's office.

In states where they are allowed, Quaker parrots are the largest of the frequently escaped companion hookbills (budgies, lovebirds, cockatiels, and Quakers). Of that group, they are also usually the most easily recovered. Since hand-fed domestic Quakers have always received their food only from humans, they are usually completely dependent upon humans to provide food and water. "Recapturing" a hand-fed Quaker parrot is, therefore, no more complicated than reaching the bird and offering food or giving the step-up command.

When a hand-fed domestic Quaker flies away, work quickly and try to keep the bird in sight. If we stay with the bird, when it decides to go to someone, we will be there, and the bird will come to us.

An escaped hand-fed Quaker parrot usually goes to a human by dark the first or second evening it is out. By the second day, the lost Quaker should be very hungry and very ready to find a friendly human.

Even the nastiest Quaker is often quite pleasant to a human who takes it in from the hostile, scary, and sometimes cold outdoors. There is occasionally a temptation on the part of a human finding the bird to simply keep it. Rescuers are sometimes knowledgeable enough to be judgmental about an owner who doesn't trim the bird's wing feathers. Depending upon the owner's intentions and practices, this might be a justifiable criticism. It is, therefore, important for the owner to report the missing bird to police and animal control and to offer a reward for the bird's return. This demonstrates the owner's honorable intentions and dedication toward the bird.

A Quaker that wants to be, can be, really, really charming. If the bird is being very sweet to its newly chosen human, we might even have to offer a reward that exceeds its material value to get the bird back.

A sample flyer for use in finding a lost companion Quaker.

If we lose sight of the bird, everything is much more complicated. When we don't know where the bird is, the whole project becomes a public relations job. We must advertise that the bird has been lost, offering a reward for its return. Brightly colored flyers posted around the neighborhood are much more effective than white ones. Newspaper advertising, including both area-wide and neighborhood press, is often very effective.

I suggest advertising at least a $50 to $100 reward for the bird's return and small rewards for any information about the bird's whereabouts. For the latter purpose, I carry $2 bills when tracking a bird. These bills are a novelty, and the children treasure them, but be sure to give money to children only in the presence of their parents.

Quaker in a Quagmire

No state supports such a large naturalized Quaker population as Florida, and no responsible parrot owner wants to further complicate this situation. It was with this serious concern—above and beyond that of losing a beloved companion—that a brave woman in Orlando, Florida, worked to recover her lost Quaker parrot during the week of the American Federation of Aviculture Convention in Tampa, 2002.

By the time Julie reached me by phone, her bird had been out for two muggy August days. Julie sounded frightened and helpless, as she talked about Cece, a two-year-old hand-fed bird, and about their daily routine, including breakfast, shower, and dressing rituals. She was especially frustrated by the site her bird had chosen to explore—an inaccessible patch of swampy, wooded wetlands across a small lake from their apartment home.

"Get outside and make noise," I suggested. "Cece wants to find you as much as you want to find her. Parrots have no innate sense of direction. That's why they have loud voices. They navigate with their ears. If you're out there in plain sight making lots of noise so that Cece knows where you are, when she's ready for something to eat, she'll come looking for her regular food source—you. Then she'll spend the day with her face in the food bowl."

Julie was obviously exhausted, not yet ready to give up, but thinking about it. When you can't even get near the tree your bird is sitting in, it's easy to think that you'll never see her again. Julie perked up when she heard confidence in my voice, and when she heard that her bird was looking for her, too. And she did get outside.

She called with an update after dark.

"Cece flew back across the lake at sunset. She's sitting in the tree beside my apartment building!" Now Julie sounded hopeful, almost confident.

"Everything is on track," I said. "She's trying to 'roost' with her 'flock,' getting as close as possible to you before dark. All you have to do is sit outside in the morning in your pajamas and eat breakfast, and you've got her. I'll have to leave for the AFA Convention by that time, but I'm speaking on recapture. Please bring her to the Convention for the talk on Sunday."

"I ... I had planned to come, but would Cece be allowed?" Julie was almost speechless, knowing that pet birds aren't usually welcome at this event.

At that moment, Cece was as good as home. *Julie* had changed! It was no longer a matter of, "*Will* I get my bird back?" Now it was, "*When* I get my bird back, will it be admitted to the convention?"

"Of course, she will. She'll be the star of the show, the demo bird that goes with my talk."

Thankfully, all went well. The next morning, Cece came right down to breakfast at the foot of the tree. I did get to hold and kiss that darling Quaker parrot in Tampa. I was humbled and honored to be allowed to say, "I told you so," right down to the part about Cece spending the first day home with her face in the food bowl.

Children are absolutely the most diligent and vigilant scouts in finding a loose pet bird flying around the neighborhood. If we can keep the children in the area looking for the bird, we have eyes everywhere.

Not everyone who finds a lost companion parrot is honest. It's not uncommon for a less-than-scrupulous stranger holding the lost Quaker "for ransom" to have an exaggerated notion of the bird's actual material value. I like to mention on the flyer that the bird is somehow imperfect, and therefore not espe-cially valuable. With an older bird I might say that the bird is known to attack or that it has daily medical needs. I believe information of this nature can generate faster and more reasonable responses if the bird has fallen into unscrupulous hands.

If we know where the bird is, and it is in a high, inaccessible place, we can sometimes lure it down with a like bird, food, or jealousy. Some-times the presence of the person the Quaker parrot hates most will bring the bird down sooner than the presence of the most beloved person.

Food dish is lowered on movable shelf until the bird must enter the cage to get the food and a human waiting out of sight pulls the door closed with a wire.

Especially if the favorite person is expressing affection to the most hated rival, the bird will sometimes come down more quickly because of jealousy than hunger.

If the bird must be lured to fly from a tree, be sure to stand facing the bird with the wind blowing against the back of your head. The bird must be able to jump into the wind in order to take off in a particular direction.

If you have to climb a tree or other structure to get close enough to reach the bird, be sure to take a pillowcase with you. It's hard enough to hold onto an angry Quaker, much less climb with one. Just tie the pillowcase in a knot to contain the bird and drop it carefully to a helper on the ground. If you must climb, be particularly careful when using metal ladders around power lines. Electrocution is probably the most common cause of death or serious injury in an accident occurring during pet bird recapture. The safest possible climbing accessory is a cherry picker, a large piece of tree-trimming equipment used by a professional operator.

Avoid the use of water hoses for the purpose of capturing a free-flying Quaker; these birds are excellent fliers, even when wet. It's highly unlikely that a good-flying Quaker can be prevented from flying with water from a garden hose, and the pressure of water from a firefighter's hose could kill the bird. On the other hand, those huge "Supersoaker" water guns can shoot a stream of water up to 50 feet (15 m). If it's dark or the bird is tiring, it can sometimes be "herded" or harassed to lower and lower places with the water gun.

Although capturing a tame hand-fed Quaker might be as easy as walking up and saying *Step up!* recapturing an experienced, human-wary wild-caught Quaker can seem a gargantuan task. The easiest way to capture a good-flying, human-shy bird is to first establish a food dependency, then trap the bird. A trap can be easily made from a man-ufactured parrot cage lying on its back with a movable wire rack that can first be situated at the (top) door to the cage. Place food first on a white dish on top of the cage. Each day, move the shelf lower into the cage. Within a few days, the bird will have to go into the cage to get the food, and the door can be pulled closed, trapping the bird inside.

Behavioral Intervention

If humans in the environment are being repeatedly outsmarted by a

Learning a New Dance

If a couple spends years dancing the fox trot and then wants to learn to tango, it's unlikely that those two particular people can learn such a radically different dance together. This couple has history, muscle memory. When they dance, it will be the way they have always danced—automatically.

However, if they each learn to tango from a separate partner, then there's a chance that they can learn to do that dance together. The presence of the experienced outsider is an important part of the process, for only after they learn from the outsider will their actions together go beyond what they were before.

---

cantankerous little tyrant Quaker parrot, professional behavioral intervention might make a world of difference. Amazingly, a Quaker that cannot be touched by anyone in the house will often prove perfectly cooperative with a professional stranger. Sometimes, only one session with a parrot behavior consultant can turn a monster into the parrot/dragon version of a saint. Owners may be stunned, moved to tears, and comment that they "don't recognize" or "don't know" that precious creature (with just a tiny remnant of yesterday's blood on the tip of its beak).

Look for a professional parrot behavior consultant with Quaker experience. Ask a reliable avian professional—a veterinarian, breeder, or other Quaker owner—for a local referral for an in-home consultation. If there is no competent local behavioral counselor to provide help for a misbehaving Quaker, telephone counseling, although more time consuming, can be a reasonable alternative. If you must depend upon telephone counseling for behavioral intervention for a Quaker parrot, be sure that the bird behaviorist works in a state where Quakers are legal so that that person will have a body of hands-on Quaker experience from which to draw. Since there is little formal education in the area of managing companion Quaker behavior, I believe the consultant with the most Quaker experience will be most likely able to successfully adjust the bird's behavior.

Expect the consultant to take a behavioral history and evaluation to determine what changes are needed and how to generate them. Then, an objective outsider with a little more experience and a little extra attention to technique can often teach Quaker owners to defeat unappealing behavior in a matter of minutes.

We must carefully evaluate both the bird and the bird's surroundings to determine whether something is missing in the bird's physical or behavioral environment. The bird might have simply learned to get attention with inappropriate behavior. A normal, stubborn animal might be confusing the owner with incomprehensible behavioral messages. The bird might have been poorly

Food rewards may be accepted from any trainer.

socialized as a nestling or only slightly socialized as a baby. It might be in an inappropriate or under stimulating environment. In any event, the bird is trying to accomplish something with its behavior.

Most companion Quakers respond dependably to predictable environmental or handling manipulations: rewards, bathing, eye games, step-up training, petting, exercises, etc. Once favorable behaviors are generated, they must be reinforced. Behaviors receiving sensitive intermittent reinforcement usually become redundant, habitual behavior.

Depending upon the bird's age, we probably have a window of opportunity of two to seven days to repeat and reinforce introduced changes. If the bird returns to exactly the same physical and behavioral environment, the behavior will return to what it was before. This likelihood increases with increased age in the bird.

Although the bird's behavior isn't actually "permanently" changed by behavioral intervention, the benefit of demonstrating immediate change can be the turning point in the attitudes of humans who create the environment. Because behavior is difficult to change, "quick fixes" used to demonstrate what a companion bird is capable of may be the best way to convince humans that if they change *their* ways, *the bird's* behavior will also change. That's a bigger *if* than it sounds. It's a real temptation for a behavioral counselor to train the bird and stop, but if humans are not adequately trained, the intervention may be unsuccessful, even though the bird responded perfectly.

Humans working to improve companion Quaker behavior must also understand that a behavior cannot be eliminated, but, rather, a behavior must be replaced with a different behavior. That is, a bird that is biting when given the step-up command cannot simply *not* bite. It can, however, replace the biting behavior with a well-patterned and accurately executed step-up command (in a Quaker, this is often accompanied by a verbal *Step up!* from the bird).

Behavior isn't linear; that is, it comes and goes. A behavior that is being eliminated will not suddenly stop. It will stop (in response to behavioral manipulation), then reappear, then stop, then reappear. If the behavioral intervention is working properly, each reappearance of the unwanted behavior will be of shorter duration and less intensity. There will be an ever-increasing number of happiness behaviors, and the unwanted behavior will gradually disappear.

Abuse

Some abuse of companion parrots by humans is intentional and meant to hurt the bird. In my opinion, however, the vast majority of abuse of companion parrots by humans is probably unintended and perpetrated in the name of "teasing," "play," or "punishment." Most humans probably have a family heritage of owning companion mammals (usually cats and dogs) or raising children. Each of these types of experiences are with creatures that have evolved as predators, so their responses differ from the responses we would expect to see from a prey species such as a Quaker parrot.

"Playing" as Abuse

Bouncing a rubber toy on a string moved rapidly in front of a normal kitten's face will provoke a pounce—an act of hunting. This behavior shows well-being in a kitten, a predator. Birds, however, are prey species, as can be observed from their eyes situated on the sides of their heads rather than in the front. Instead of the instinct to hunt, these creatures have an instinct to fight or fly, with an accent on the fly. Because they must be able to escape from predators, these prey species have developed the ability to see almost 360 degrees around the head rather than merely see the area in front of the head.

Given the opportunity, when threatened, most birds probably prefer to fly away from danger. In a bird such as a healthy companion Quaker parrot with trimmed wing feathers, if the bird cannot fly away, the instinct to fight will dominate the instinct to fly. This might make it seem that a provoked Quaker parrot that is defending itself or its territory is enjoying jousting with the broom handle or golf club. Actually, the strong emotional reaction (fear) that the bird is feeling is probably quite unlike the emotions felt by a kitten in the act of hunting (joy). Defending its territory from a large predator may indicate health on the bird's part, but it is a stress reaction, not a happiness behavior. Therefore, provoking a Quaker parrot to defend its territory (a stress reaction) is ultimately destructive to the bird's health and personality, and is, therefore, abusive.

Even the gentlest Quaker parrot may respond to insensitive handling with nips or even bites.

Provoking the Quaker Parrot to Chase

While some Quaker parrots appear to relish chasing people away from the cage, I believe this behavior is also a stress reaction. Anyone repeatedly racing past the cage can cause recurrent stress reactions and ultimately harm the bird. Therefore, if family pets, children, or others frequently rush past the cage, stimulating either fear, thrashing, chasing, or attacking in the bird, the cage should be relocated. If people frequently rush through a doorway, it can seem to the bird that they are magically appearing out of thin air. The cage should be moved or humans should move more slowly or call out if they are about to come through the doorway.

Humans who intentionally provoke a Quaker parrot to chase must be advised that their behavior is abusive. An adult who is teasing or provoking a Quaker parrot can easily choose to stop. If children or companion animals are abusing the Quaker parrot, they are probably best denied access to the bird (especially if the bird is also "abusing" them). If these situations cannot be quickly remedied, the bird should be removed from the home.

Repeatedly provoking a bird to bite can be behaviorally damaging in many ways.

Punishment

The Quaker parrot is a willful and determined animal. It is a wild, undomesticated creature that cannot help but use the tools nature gave it. A human who cannot tolerate an occasional bite is probably not cut out to be a parrot owner. Hitting the cage, throwing things at the cage, blowing smoke in the cage, or spraying anything but a mist of water (rainfall) at the bird can very quickly damage the bird. Hitting a Quaker parrot, "thumping" it on the beak, throwing the bird on the floor, or against the wall, can easily injure or kill the bird. A nipping Quaker is most successfully patterned using the techniques and responses described in this book, handled more, or moved to a more empathetic environment.

I occasionally encounter people who have withheld food from a Quaker parrot because they have been bitten. This is especially cruel, as a Quaker parrot can't understand that it is hungry today because it bit someone yesterday.

I once did an in-home for an "aggressive Quaker parrot" where the owner admitted that the bird had been given no food since biting about ten days before my visit. When I advised that the bird should be immediately given food, the

owner proceeded to fill the bowl with black oil sunflower seeds (the kind bought cheaply at the grocery store for feeding wild birds), the bird's exclusive diet. Not only had this particular owner figured out how to overtly abuse the bird by withholding food, he had destroyed the bird's health by feeding it a grossly inadequate diet. Obviously, the bird didn't have much energy by the time of my visit, as it had survived by eating the shells from the sunflower seeds (and who knows what else) foraged from the bottom of the cage. I recommended placing the bird for adoption.

Neglect

Failure to feed for behavioral reasons is, unfortunately, a common scenario for a Quaker parrot that is about to be given away. If the owner has decided that the bird is incompatible or untrainable, it might not be fed again in that home. This is especially common in situations where the bird has been banished to a basement or backroom because it is noisy, messy, or otherwise unappreciated. Obviously, the bird must be removed from the home immediately.

It is not uncommon for such a bird to consume surprising amounts of food during the first few hours in the new or foster home. If food deprivation has been ongoing for some time, the bird might have physical problems related to chronic malnutrition or might develop a permanent behavioral problem with overeating. A chronic

A Quaker parrot that is allowed access to chocolate, coffee, or other enticing but toxic foods is being abused.

overeater must be carefully monitored to avoid obesity.

Secret Abuse

A Quaker parrot that suddenly attacks a certain adult, child, or other companion animal is probably not responding to secret abuse. However, suddenly becoming fearful and avoiding a child or human might indicate that secret abuse is occurring when the human and bird are alone. Multiple subtle behavioral changes such as overeating, thrashing, fearfulness, discontinuing talking, increased vocalization, avoiding a particular individual, or ripping out feathers only in that individual's presence could be signs of secret abuse.

It's time to spend a few moments investigating the source of the behavioral changes. In some cases, the bird might be the subject of secret abuse, but this is not always, or even often, the case; in most cases it is probably no more than a temporary response to an accidental behavior. Feather chewing, especially, is a very complex physical and/or behavioral

A Quaker parrot should be encouraged to interact with many different individuals, including close friends and strangers.

Temporary Foster Care

Many life changes and transitions are temporary. If it seems that a situation will improve, it's comforting to know that the bird can come home some day. For this purpose, I like to encourage Quaker parrot owners to allow their birds to have relationships with an appropriate foster parent or family. This can provide a Quaker parrot with potential vacation housing, improved relationships as a result of balanced bonding, and a place to stay during times of personal transition.

"Permanent" Adoption

If the situation creating abuse for a Quaker parrot is not going to change, a long-term adoption is necessary. Because of what the bird has been through and the behavioral responses to those problems, a potential owner should not be expected to pay anything resembling a retail price; however, the new owner should be expected to pay for veterinary evaluation and any behavioral and physical rehabilitation. If the new adoptive owner has an appropriate cage, the bird should be given *without charge* to the new owner. If the new adoptive owner does not have an appropriate cage and the current owner does, then the current owner might suggest a modest price for the bird's cage and accessories.

condition that does not, in itself, indicate that a bird is being abused. Some of the most pampered, obviously unabused birds in the world chew their feathers.

Scapegoating

Not all of life goes as we expect, and nothing ever stays the same. Difficulties in human relationships can sometimes result in the Quaker parrot being blamed for human issues. If the bird is either causing human problems such as pain, allergies, or sleeplessness, or if it is being blamed for human problems, especially if physical or emotional abuse is occurring in the home, the bird must be removed from the home immediately.

Chapter Seven
The Perfect Imperfects

Among the most cherished of all companion Quaker parrots are those called "imperfects" in the feather fancy. These birds have survived injuries resulting in temporary or permanent disfigurement. They may be available for free or for contribution to their medical expenses. In some, the damage is merely cosmetic; in others, injuries result in reduced capabilities. The plucky Quaker parrot is capable of surviving extremely disfiguring injuries. Some Quakers have been so badly injured that they have lost important skills such as the ability to walk, fly, climb, see, or eat, yet they have survived to become happy, successful companions.

Recoverable Injuries

Many of these injuries occur in the nest box, during hand-feeding, or fledging. While some of the injuries to baby Quaker parrots are permanently disfiguring, it is not unusual for a baby Quaker to completely recover from injuries incurred before weaning. Recoverable imperfections include feather-chewed head or back, burned or punctured crop, chewed-off toenails, or spraddle leg (see page 90) discovered within the first few days of life. The baby bird will usually regrow feathers on the chewed head or back right away.

Damaged crop. This can occur when a baby Quaker is being hand-fed and formula is either too hot or has hot spots because it was not stirred well. If the injury is not sutured, the baby will probably die. If a baby Quaker survives a burned crop, and the crop was sutured, the adult bird will probably retain no visible signs of the injury. Occasionally, the bird may have some discomfort where the crop and skin over the crop adhere. A badly burned crop

Many companion parrots function normally with missing or less than perfect toes.

This Quaker parrot as a nestling lost some or all of every toe.

hobbles or a technique involving pulling the baby's legs down through a customized sponge. These devices hold the baby's legs in a corrective position as it grows while allowing it to use the legs and develop muscles. The bird's legs will stay under it in adulthood.

Uncorrected spraddle leg. This might result in the affected leg being "frozen" in an almost unusable position out to the side of the body. These birds must be supplied with an environment especially designed to accommodate their injuries—perhaps by living in a carpeted aquarium, a short, padded box, or a cage with horizontal bars.

Cosmetic Imperfections

Loss of toenails. Many injuries resulting in permanent disfigurement don't interfere in the bird's ability to function normally in captivity. One of the most common of these injuries in Quaker parrots is the loss of toenails, a common injury among parrots that are shipped or housed in groups. It is also sometimes observed as a nest box injury, as parent Quakers may occasionally chew one or more toenails off babies in the nest box. Two or fewer missing toes or toenails are hardly a handicap for a Quaker parrot.

Wings, beaks, eyes. Occasionally, a Quaker parrot might have suffered an injury resulting in crooked or missing wings, a malformed beak, or

might require suturing more than once. Rarely, one or two feathers covering the crop might grow in the wrong direction on the adult bird.

Punctured crop. This is a similar, usually less severe injury that can result perhaps from using cedar chips in the nest box or brooder. Or, a baby Quaker might occasionally puncture its crop with a toy or with the clasp that attaches the toy to the cage. Because there is less damage and the skin at the edges of the wound is stronger, this type of injury is usually easier to treat and heals more quickly than a burned crop. With appropriate veterinary care, Quaker parrots usually recover completely from this kind of injury.

Spraddle leg. Some baby Quakers are hatched with or develop splayed legs. If recognized early, it can usually be partially or fully corrected. The veterinarian may use asymmetrical eyes. While these injuries might be glaring imperfections, they might not interfere with a Quaker parrot's ability to function normally as a companion to humans. Slightly damaged wings that remove the capacity for flight might be fatal to a wild Quaker parrot. In an indoor-living situation, however, a Quaker parrot with this kind of injury may be able to have a beautiful set of full wing feathers with no danger of flying away.

One of the most commonly seen beak malformations is scissor beak in which the upper mandible and lower mandible are offset to opposite sides. This and some other minor malformations of the beak can sometimes be corrected by massaging or filing the beak into shape. If the bird can crack seed and eat independently, this is really no disability at all. I believe I see anecdotal evidence to suggest that parrots with minor beak deformities may be less susceptible to the development of feather chewing and self-mutilation syndrome.

Imperfections Impairing Abilities

More severe imperfections may require environmental and handling accommodations such as padded surfaces, wide, flat-topped perches, cages with horizontal bars, or special diets. Perhaps the most common of these is the Quaker parrot that is missing all its toes. Again, this is a nest box injury usually caused

Loss of a foot or leg can affect a bird's ability to function.

by a parent bird. Although it is generally believed that parents that remove feathers from the babies' heads and backs are eager to go to nest again and are merely "persuading" the current babies to leave the nest, this does not appear to be the source of the behavior of removing the babies' toes. A small amount of anecdotal evidence suggests that removing toes may occur more frequently in pairs that breed in nest boxes only rather than weaving some sort of nest or a woven nest in and/or around the nest box.

Colorado breeder Ginger Eldon had a Quaker parrot pair that produced perfect babies in a nest box with a woven millet stem nest. Later, when they went to nest without weaving the millet stem nest inside the nest box, they neatly chewed off all the toes (up to about the first joint) from the feet of two clutches of babies. After that, Ginger incubated the pairs' nine eggs per clutch and hand-fed the babies from day one.

Don't Forget the Bow

One Fourth of July I was called upon to take a one-legged Quaker with a broken leg to the veterinarian. The poor young bird had reacted with great fear upon its first exposure to the sounds of fireworks. Since Colorado is a state that requires banding, the bird's only leg was banded, and, apparently, the band was caught on something in the cage when the bird thrashed in fear in response to nearby explosions.

What a sad sight that little critter was, holding on to the side of the cage with her beak. The owner was consumed with grief and guilt. He vowed never to touch another firecracker.

Dr. Jerry LaBonde removed the bird's band and set her leg in a tiny little splint. He advised me that the bird should stay in an aquarium for a couple of weeks, and that she should have lots of padded horizontal ladders to sit on in the

Peg recovered completely from having broken her only leg.

future. Dr. LaBonde was just about to put her back into the cage, when he stopped and looked, and said, "Oh, my, I nearly forgot the bow!"

"Bow?" I asked. "You need a bow on a Quaker's splint?"

"That's the most important part," the good doctor replied as he double-knotted a tiny gauze bow. "I call them 'teasers.' If the bow sticks out and maybe moves around a little bit, the bird will chew on the bow and leave the splint alone."

At this writing, the Eldons still had two Quakers with chewed-off toes from those clutches. When they were babies, carpet was provided on the bottom of the cage of these birds, but now they function as normal adults (even to the point of copulation) in an ordinary cage. These birds still have a little of every toe, but Quakers with only little round feet with absolutely no toes often do just as well.

Quakers raised around larger birds must be carefully supervised and meticulously housed to prevent altercations. Quaker parrots involved in altercations with larger birds might end up missing one foot or leg (or more). A Quaker parrot missing only one foot or leg can still get around pretty well, especially if easy climbing opportunities are provided. Many ladders, flat perches, and horizontal bars should be included that allow the bird to use its beak as a second foot.

Extreme Imperfections

A Quaker parrot that attacks a larger bird may come away from the encounter with no beak. This type of injury may involve only the upper mandible, in which case the beak can occasionally be reattached by an experienced avian veterinarian. Even those birds missing both the upper and lower parts of the beak often learn to eat independently by scooping foods that don't have to be cracked or chewed. Warm cereals such as grits and oatmeal are excellent for this purpose. Small pieces of fresh fruits and vegetables sprinkled with generous amounts of a good-quality ground pelleted diet can be very effective in providing balanced nutrition for the bird. Loss of the beak may not impair talking ability, although it might affect the motivation to speak.

Blindness: Cataracts in Quakers are rare, but we see occasional blindness in them. Even birds that are completely sightless often learn to adjust to their cage, probably through trial-and-error, sound, and vibrations. In these cases, owners should seldom make any changes in the bird's environment. A Quaker parrot with sight in only one eye is more common. In this case, we must approach the bird only from the sighted side to avoid either fearful or aggressive responses.

Imperfect Quaker parrots can develop very accommodating personalities.

Missing extremities: The extremely adaptable Quaker parrot is well known to survive even some very devastating injuries such as missing both feet or legs. Again, a carpeted aquarium or very short-sided box is good for housing these birds; a footless or legless Quaker should not be in a box with high sides it can't see over. According to Dr. Jerry LaBonde, a Quaker parrot housed in a too tall box might feel that it's in a hole and develop related behavior problems.

Behavior

The most significant thing about physically imperfect companion Quaker parrots is that they often develop extremely accommodating, cooperative personalities almost naturally. If a rare behavior problem does develop, it is usually corrected—as in the "perfect" Quaker parrot—with enhanced environment or increased handling. Interestingly, physically imperfect Quakers are often considered by their owners to be "absolutely perfect" in every way.

Chapter Eight

Family Issues

Children and Quaker Parrots

Because a Quaker parrot is sturdier than a budgie, lovebird, or cockatiel, and yet small enough to do little real damage to a child, it can be a good choice as a companion for a child. There is great potential for highly complementary relationships between Quakers and children, especially between only Quakers and only children. Unfortunately, there is also potential for Quaker parrots and children to abuse one another.

The best candidates for juvenile Quaker owners are tolerant, responsible children who are usually at least six to eight years old. Of course, this

consideration is highly subjective and depends completely upon the bird and the child. Some very young children have been able to develop and maintain excellent relationships with Quaker parrots. One two-year-old might do very well with a particular Quaker, and a teenager might not do well with the very same bird, or vice versa.

Careful training of children to perform step-up practice, and adult supervision of the development of the authority-based relationship are necessary to ensure a peaceful Quaker/child relationship. The bird must be patterned to demonstrate the same cooperative behaviors with the child as it would with the child's parent. It is especially important to instruct a child not to teach the bird to chase by running away from it. A timid, fearful child who retreats or runs from the bird can actually provoke a Quaker parrot to more abusive behavior.

Because a Quaker parrot can perceive children and shorter people as worthy of abuse, children should be taught to give the step-up command from a higher position. That is, never try to "hand" a Quaker parrot from a taller person to a shorter one,

but, rather, place the bird in a lower position than the person who wishes to handle the bird. The easiest way to do this is to place the bird on the floor so that even the shortest person can easily accomplish a successful step up.

It is usually difficult for a child to persuade an established Quaker parrot to step up from inside the cage. Instead, children may be taught to give the step-up command to a Quaker parrot that has come out of the cage and is sitting on the top of the cage or cage door. If a child wishes to step up a Quaker parrot from the cage top or door, again, teach him or her to stand on a stool, ladder, or chair in order to be in a height-dominant position. This should stimulate the bird to cooperate. If the bird is nippy at the cage, the child might provide a hand-held perch rather than a hand, assuming that the bird is appropriately patterned to step up to a perch as described previously. Of course, the child should also participate in step-up practice, outings, and, especially, all behavioral practices designed to balance bonding (see Balancing Bonding in Chapter Four).

A child must always be able to expect help and support from adults in providing adequate care, including annual veterinary exams, for any companion animal. Adults should also regularly examine and trim wing feathers to prevent the loss of the bird from flying-related accidents.

Children should be supervised, counseled, and sometimes reminded

A Quaker parrot with well-formed physical and emotional territories might not take kindly to the introduction of a human baby.

to leave the toilet lid down so that the bird will not drown in the toilet. Children must not sleep with these friendly birds and must also be careful not to close them in drawers and doors.

Infants and Quaker Parrots

An established Quaker parrot in the home might not take kindly to the introduction of a noisy rival that smells funny, has more toys, eats more often, and gets more of Mom's or Dad's attention than the bird does. A Quaker parrot is more likely to grow truculent, noisy, and aggressive than to sulk, stop eating, or become depressed. These tendencies can be moderated by preparing the bird for the new baby's arrival and by providing sensitive supervision, shared

Let the Quaker parrot meet the baby's toys before it meets the baby.

attention, and positive reinforcement after the baby comes home.

Early Preparation

Preparing for a new human baby calls for increased patterning and handling a companion Quaker at exactly the time when expectant humans might be naturally tempted to handle the bird less. Any time a Quaker parrot receives less attention, it will naturally begin behaving in ways designed to attract attention, which might mean making more noise with its voice or with its toys. This is the worst possible time to neglect regular step-up practice.

At least three months before the baby arrives, begin introducing baby accessories into the home. Show the bird the toys for the baby and provide a similar, Quaker-appropriate toy for each toy that the baby will have (at least at first). Later, toys can be periodically

rotated and reintroduced to the Quaker parrot as "new."

Introduce the Quaker parrot to all the baby's new things, using language that lets the bird know that the baby is "connected" to the bird and to the family. Using the baby's name (or the word "Baby") and the bird's name in tandem, is often effective in establishing this behavioral tradition (pattern). When showing the baby's things to the bird, we might say, "This is Paco's baby's new toy, and this is baby's Paco's new toy."

Well in advance of the baby's arrival, begin sharing attention with the Quaker parrot and a baby doll. Introduce the bird and the baby, again using the names in tandem. Cuddle and interact with the baby doll exactly as you would with the newborn, and show the bird how to interact peacefully with the new baby.

When the New Baby Comes Home

It's only natural that the new parents' attentions will be overwhelmingly directed toward the baby, but efforts should be made to find a little energy for the bird, too. The key to appropriate Quaker parrot behavior during this period might be Dad. If Mom is usually the primary Quaker parrot care provider, then Dad might take over those duties and forge new bonds with the bird.

This is a good time to invite friends of the bird over to visit and handle it. This can also be an excellent opportunity for the bird to spend some time

Mommy, I'm SO Smart

I was taking a shower. It was too late for Guido to get in with me, so I put his T-bar perch between the bathroom and hallway and placed him on it.

Guido loves to imitate animal calls and sounds. When practicing his repertoire, I'll hear him say things like:

What's kitty cat say? Meow!

What's chicken say? Bruck, bruck!

What's turkey say? Gobble, gobble!

What's puppy say? Bark, bark!

What's cow say? Mooooooooo!

While in the shower, I wondered what he would say if I asked him what Bilbo (my Himalayan) said. So I asked.

Guido, what's Bilbo say?

Silence. He was thinking. Hard.

I said, *Guido, Bilbo's a kitty cat. So, what's Bilbo say.*

I instantly heard *Meow!*

I was thrilled. Could he have possibly associated Bilbo with being a kitty cat; therefore, of course, he said, *Meow?*

I waited a few moments, then asked. *Guido, what's Bilbo say?*

Again, *Meow!*

I told him what a smart bird he was. I noticed that Bilbo was sitting on the floor, almost eye-level with Guido and his perch, purring loudly.

Again, I asked the question. *Guido, what does Bilbo say?*

The answer I received this time was *Bye-bye!*

As I turned to Guido to tell him, *No, Sweetie, that's not what Bilbo...,* I noticed that Bilbo was leaving with Guido watching as he ran down the stairs. I guess his response really *was* appropriate.

Mommy was wrong.

Tena M. Marangi
Alexandria, Virginia

with grandparents or some other extended family. If no other alternative home is available, the Quaker parrot might benefit from being boarded for the first few weeks while the human parents attach and adjust to their new offspring. Even if there is no alternative home available, the bird will benefit from excursions in the car or to other safe, indoor environments like the bank, the shopping mall, the veterinarian, or the groomer.

Whenever possible the Quaker parrot should share attention and interactions with the parents in the presence of the baby. While a Quaker parrot might not be actually handled at the same time a baby is being handled—for reasons of hygiene—we can talk to the bird as we talk to the baby. Modeling talking behavior for a human baby and a Quaker parrot establishes a natural model/rival situation that can enhance the learning process for both human and bird.

When there's a new human infant in the home, we can prevent

the development of attention-demanding behaviors in our companion Quaker parrot with the generous use of *positive reinforcement* for any appropriate behavior. It's probably also a good idea to ask friends to say "Hi" to or greet the bird before coming over to coo over the baby. Continue using the bird's and the baby's names in tandem through the baby's first year to help the bird accept the child.

Keep the Bird and the New Baby on the Same Schedule

The bird and the baby should eat, sleep, and bathe at approximately the same times. Simultaneous feeding is especially helpful in preventing the development of attention-demanding behaviors at this time. Human babies must eat frequently. Quaker parrots perceive eating as a social interaction. Feed the Quaker parrot at least a little something every time you feed the baby, or serious jealousy behaviors could develop. Likewise, offer a bowl of water for the Quaker to bathe in whenever bathing the baby. Of course, you must insist that the bird and the baby sleep at the same times.

Provide the Quaker parrot with opportunities for wing-flapping exercise to help it to express excess energy that might develop during this exciting time in a young family's life. It's probably not a good idea to add a new Quaker parrot, or any other pet, when a new baby has just arrived, as both creatures will require a great deal of attention.

Quaker Parrots and Other Pets

Because Quaker parrots are so social, breeding in extremely close proximity not only to other Quakers, but also sharing the nests with other species, it might be said that the Quaker parrot is the only parrot that "keeps pets" in the wild. In captivity, Quaker parrots may develop highly compatible relationships with other pets, as well as highly adversarial relationships. Supervising a new Quaker/pet relationship, understanding Quaker "culture," and reinforcing appropriate behavior for an approved neighbor is necessary to ensure complementary relationships with other pets. A carefully timed clap, squirt, or bop on the too-interested nose will pattern the other pet to avoid predatory behavior.

Sharing a toy outside the cage can make or break a Quaker parrot friendship.

Like other parrots, Quakers may violently defend a bond to a location or a human and jealously abuse others, including pets, that might be perceived as intruders into their territory. Locating the cage well away from traffic areas is probably crucial here, for if a particular animal rushes frequently past the Quaker parrot cage, it might stimulate and pattern chasing behaviors in the bird.

Prepare to introduce a new pet into the home of an established Quaker in much the same way as preparing for a new human baby, by telling the Quaker parrot that the new addition is coming and by sensitively supervising their introduction. Always intervene if the Quaker parrot seems to be trying to chase or attack.

Although a Quaker parrot is much more likely to be killed by a dog than by a cat, caring owners know that their cats must be well socialized as kittens. Some Quaker owners even feel that a cat's front claws should be removed if there is a bird in the house. In most cases this is probably unnecessary; I have seen no cases of cats killing Quakers.

It is not unusual for a Quaker parrot to repeatedly attack a dog. It is especially unwise to trust a Quaker parrot alone with such a dog, for if the bird has abused the dog repeatedly in the past, some day that dog will defend itself, and there might not be much of the bird left.

While most Quakers do well with most cats, ferrets are especially deadly to small birds. I do not recom-

mend adding a Quaker or any other small parrot to a home with a ferret.

Quakers cannot usually be trusted with either larger or smaller birds. Carefully supervise any interaction in which a larger animal interacts with a smaller one, especially if the Quaker parrot is the larger animal. Quaker parrots can be a threat to smaller creatures in the home such as insects, spiders, lizards, reptiles, mice, hamsters, and gerbils.

Quaker parrots might or might not be compatible with an additional Quaker parrot in the home.

Quaker parrots can be a threat to smaller animals in the home.

Chapter Nine
Rehabilitation

The Previously Owned Quaker Parrot

For a person seeking a free or very inexpensive bird, opportunities abound to rehabilitate previously owned Quaker parrots. While many birds, especially older wild-caught or recaptured ferals, offer only limited companion potential, young adoption or resale hand-fed birds are good candidates to become quality companions.

Even well-behaved Quaker parrots in perfect feather may be available for adoption.

The Physical Rehabilitation Process

An adoption or resale Quaker parrot with good companion potential is probably no more than two or three years old. Radically improved behavior is possible at any age, but it is especially easy at this age. This is a common time for an unsocialized Quaker to be bounced to a second home. A Quaker parrot that has not been handled can become a real tyrant in its home territory. Moving the bird will make a big difference.

While the Quaker parrot is not usually a shy creature, changing homes can be unsettling for even the most cantankerous animal. If the bird was not socialized to accept change, the move could be extremely unsettling. The perceived drastic changes provided by coming to a new home usually provide a window of opportunity for reinforcing good behavior during the temporary period of adjustment. This is similar to the "honeymoon period" experienced by baby hand-feds coming into the first home, but the window of opportunity for reinforcing good behavior is brief. You must work quickly and decisively to make the most of this fleeting opportunity.

An adoption Quaker may not have had the best care, so begin the physical rehabilitation process by taking the bird immediately to the avian veterinarian, possibly before taking the bird home. Be sure to observe appropriate quarantine procedures as specified by the veterinarian, especially if other birds are in the home. This period will probably be at least one to three months, during which the Quaker must be behaviorally rehabilitated. If behavioral rehabilitation is not begun until after quarantine, we may have already missed the window of opportunity to easily reinforce appropriate behavior.

Ask the veterinarian to examine and update the bird's wing feather trim. This will be important in training or retraining the bird to step up. During the first few hours or days in the home, a little extra security can be provided by covering about one fourth of the cage with a towel so that the bird has a place to hide if it chooses to do so. Place the cage well out of traffic areas and a little higher than you normally might. If there are no other birds already there, situate the bird in the living area for resocialization.

If the bird can be handled, hold it as much as possible during the first 48 hours. Work on step-up patterning (see page 17) for as long as the bird seems interested or willing. Handle the bird less if it seems to tire easily, perhaps providing a little extra heat and privacy for the first few days.

When moving a Quaker parrot from one home to another, carefully examine wing feathers so that extra precautions will be taken for flighted birds.

Even though the bird should have no strongly developed instincts to defend new territory, be sure to practice step ups away from the bird's cage. Be sure also to pattern the bird to step up on a hand-held perch as well as onto hands. Never attempt step ups from the cage unless the bird is well patterned to step ups in unfamiliar territory.

A two-to-three-year-old Quaker parrot in a new home should go through a "honeymoon period" similar to the baby days followed by the terrible twos just as a baby Quaker would, but these developmental phases will be of much shorter duration. A young, adopted, domestic bird should be socialized exactly as a baby Quaker would.

The Adopted Quaker's Diet

When the bird's diagnostic tests come back, consult the veterinarian before trying to improve the bird's diet by supplementing vitamins. If the bird has a less-than-healthy liver or kidneys, be very careful about vitamin supplementation, especially with D_3, which could kill the bird. It is better to improve the diet with real food: fresh fruits, vegetables, pasta, and a quality commercial diet. Almost any food—quality whole grain toast, macaroni and cheese, or oatmeal—served warm should seem like "love" to a previously hand-fed Quaker parrot that has been neglected. Don't forget to offer minerals such as mineral blocks, cuttlebone, and oyster shell calcium.

It's not unusual for a newly adopted Quaker parrot to be addicted to seeds, especially sunflower or safflower seeds. This is similar to adopting a child that will eat only French fries. It's important to get these birds on a canary-based mix as quickly as possible; then we can begin mixing the pelleted diet with the seeds and eventually wean the bird to healthy food.

Games

As quickly as possible, the bird should be socialized to enjoy playing snuggling and peek-a-boo games in a towel. A bird that has been mishandled may be terrified of the towel. Try to use a light green towel; that would be the same color as the bird. The goal here is to replicate the feeling of security of being under Mommy's wings.

If the bird is initially afraid of the towel, try playing with the bird in the covers of the bed. Blankets may be less intimidating to a bird that has been roughly toweled.

Warning. Be sure not to fall asleep when playing snuggle games with the bird in the bed.

Wild-Caught Quakers

Because of its international status as an agricultural pest rather than a threatened or endangered species, the Quaker parrot was the last bird legally imported into the United States. The last legal wild-caught Quaker parrots entered the United States in 1993. If these birds live to their thirties, there will be older wild-caught Quaker parrots occasionally in the marketplace in the United States through the year 2023. Wild-caught Quakers will probably continue to be available outside the United States.

Although older and possibly never before socialized to human touch, a surprising number of these birds may offer good pet potential. They require the same veterinary examination and quarantine, and they experience the same stages of behavioral development as a domestic baby parrot as they acclimate to the new home. The same socialization processes used with handfeds should be used for wild-caught Quakers, but changes and advances should be made more carefully, with this exception: A new hand-fed baby Quaker parrot should be held on a limited schedule only, guiding it to learn also to play alone (develop independence). An older, bird-bonded or wild-caught Quaker parrot should be held for long periods of time to build and improve the human/Quaker bond.

Rather than beginning with touching and holding, however, the new owner should begin befriending an untamed parrot with games and passive interactions as discussed in my book, *Barron's Guide to a Well-Behaved Parrot* (see page 121). It is best to establish contact with the bird first with games involving no eye contact and progress to games involving limited eye contact. Offer food from the hand, play the Towel Game, and sleep in front of the bird before hand contact is attempted. Again, if the bird won't tolerate the Towel Game, try playing Peek-a-Bird with a blanket, bedspread, or quilt.

Many tamed, wild-caught Quakers bite less than their domestic cousins. Tamed wild-caught Quakers sometimes fail to acquire human speech, but they can be charming companions in a different, wilder way.

Old wild-caught Quakers may be available through adoption programs with bird clubs. In many cases, the only way to identify a resocialized wild-caught or feral Quaker from a resocialized hand-fed is by the open band and by the voice. A Quaker parrot that has been around wild Quaker parrots may come with a totally obnoxious voice. It may be necessary to spend more time on noise control than actual socialization, but don't neglect socialization just because a Quaker makes a little noise. A conscientiously applied program of increased handling, combined with distracting from the noise *before* it occurs and reinforcing the

introduced behavior will quickly bring noise under control.

Recaptured Feral Quakers

Some may argue that naturalized Quakers in the United States are happy living in their wild state and should be left alone. In some situations, however, there may be compelling reasons to recapture.

The birds might be living in an area where they would be subjected to extreme or adverse weather conditions, or they might be in danger of being exterminated to protect agriculture in an area where they might proliferate. Nonnative species have no legal protection, and there is no reason why a citizen, especially a farmer, couldn't kill the bird.

While a recaptured Quaker probably has the least potential of this group to learn speech, many of them adjust well to life in the living room. They will probably be addicted to seed and will probably require "taming" to get the hang of

Even wild Quaker parrots at Brooklyn College are said to seek out leftover pizza. This portion is too much for one Quaker parrot. ("Never eat anything larger than your head.")

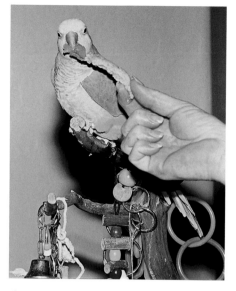

Sharing food and gentle eye games reinforces the cooperative bond.

A Quaker parrot might mourn the loss of a longtime companion.

sive interactions. Again, start with games involving no eye contact and progress to games involving limited eye contact. When it has calmed somewhat, take the wing feather-trimmed bird to a small restricted area such as a bathroom, closet, or hallway. Begin the first day by sitting on the floor with feet drawn up and knees up. Put the bird on a Quaker green towel (chartreuse) on your knees and spend an hour or so reading out loud to the bird. The second day, spend less time reading, and begin socializing with the Towel Game, progressing as quickly as possible to the step-up practice.

Even an older Quaker that has lived wild on more than one occasion will frequently tame down in minutes. Again, the biggest battles here will probably involve reducing noise and improving the diet.

When a Quaker Parrot Survives Its Owner

When a Quaker parrot survives its owner, there is usually a very brief period, usually no more than a few weeks, of silence or withdrawn behavior. A Quaker parrot that loses its owner rarely stops eating; more likely, the bird will become truculent and territorial and not allow anyone near its cage. It might call or continue looking for that favorite person. Likewise, a Quaker parrot might mourn, call, or seek out a recently deceased household pet.

This is one more time when the existence of a second or foster

the stepping-up. I have tamed and taught step ups to many such birds, and it's usually much easier than one might suppose.

As with wild-caught Quaker parrots, begin befriending an untamed Quaker parrot with games and pas-

home that is willing to become a permanent home is ideal. If the bird is already familiar with the new permanent human and new permanent home, the transition will be easier. The bird's diet and routine should remain as close as possible to the one it was before the loss. To make the transition easier, owners should provide a written record of the bird's customary diet, preferences, dislikes, and vocabulary as well as information about the bird's veterinarian, groomer, behavioral consultant, pet sitter, boarding facility, or other service providers, and any other idiosyncrasies that might affect the bird's happy adjustment in a new home. This written record might resemble the information recommended for a physical and behavioral history form in the section that follows on operating a Quaker parrot adoption program.

Owners who want to know where their birds will go if anything happens to them should make arrangements today. If there is no established foster home, or no provision for the bird in the owner's will, the bird might be placed through an adoption service.

If a Quaker parrot's owner is ill, elderly, or otherwise homebound and lives alone, it's a good idea to establish a daily "check-up" system so that someone knows that all is well in the house every day. Not only is this good for the solitary owner, it also ensures that the bird will be found should the owner fall ill or die. Because it takes only a short time for a bird to die of thirst, a check-up system is necessary to ensure its survival. This service for the elderly might be provided through a church volunteer organization or other in-home service provider; it is a noble and worthy project occasionally available through local bird clubs.

Operating a Quaker Parrot Adoption Program

It's been said before: Nobody's perfect, and nothing stays the same. Quaker parrots are frequently transferred through adoption programs in the United States. Many absolutely "normal" (probably neglected) Quaker parrots are given away through adoption programs every day. Even the best-loved companion Quaker might someday need a home.

Many local and American Federation of Aviculture affiliated clubs operate adoption placement programs, most operated by volunteers and are free of charge by donation. However, operating an adoption program can be one of the most contentious areas of any organization. Some of the most bitter disputes and misunderstandings I have ever observed have developed as a result of adoptions.

Nowhere in aviculture is there a greater need for record keeping. At least three documents are needed to complete and record each adoption:

It's a good idea to have documentation of a particular bird's food, toy, and sleeping preferences.

1. *Application to Adopt a Quaker Parrot* from a potential new owner;
2. *Physical and Behavioral History* from the current/former owner; and
3. *Transfer of Ownership* to the new owner.

When interim temporary care is needed for the bird (a foster home), five documents are required to complete transfer of ownership:

1. *Physical and Behavioral History* from the current/former owner;
2. *Transfer of Ownership* to the individual or organization supervising the adoption;
3. *Agreement for Foster Care* between the care provider and the individual or organization supervising the adoption;
4. *Application to Adopt a Quaker Parrot* from a potential new owner; and
5. *Transfer of Ownership* to the new owner.

Screening Adoptive Homes

It's a good idea to accept and review applications for potential new owners before birds become available. The following information at least should be included on an *Application for Quaker Parrot Adoption*. It's a good idea to have your organization's forms reviewed by an attorney.

- Name/Address/Day and Evening Telephone
- Please describe your previous experience with parrots.
- Have you ever owned a Quaker parrot?
- Where is that bird now?
- What other companion animals, including birds, do you now own?
- Do you now have an appropriate cage for a Quaker parrot? What are the cage dimensions?
- Have you read *Guide to a Well-Behaved Parrot* or other behavioral manuals?
- Are you willing to assume all responsibility for this bird?

- Do you intend to maintain this bird as a companion or a breeder?
- Do you have experience breeding Quakers or other parrots?
- Are you familiar with the Model Aviaries Program?
- At what date are you prepared to assume responsibility for this bird?
- Are there any additional considerations that might affect this adoption placement?

Matching the Bird to the New Home

The bird's needs and characteristics affect the home into which the bird should go. If the bird is bonded to humans, it should be placed as a companion bird. Similarly, if the bird is an egg eater, a chronic masturbator, or has abused its mate, it should be adopted as a companion not a breeder. If the bird has a history of successful breeding and failure to thrive as a companion, it should be adopted into a breeding situation.

Following are suggested considerations for the *Behavioral and Medical History* form:
- Name of Quaker parrot:
- Band number and type of band:
- Original source of the bird:
- Age/hatch date:
- Time in this household:
- Anomalies or identifying characteristics:
- Eating habits:
- Playing habits:
- Bathing habits:
- What does the bird say?

- Have you observed any extremely fearful behaviors regarding humans? Animals? Objects? Restraint?
- Preferences (foods, music, gender, color, etc.)
- Has this bird ever been injured or ill? Describe:
- Has this bird seen an avian veterinarian? Who?
- Are you willing to have veterinary records transferred?
- When was the last time the bird went to the veterinarian?
- Has the bird had any behavioral problems including shyness, screaming, biting, or self-mutilation in the past?
- Has this bird seen a behavioral consultant? Who?

Empathetic foster care can turn a misbehaving Quaker parrot's behavior around.

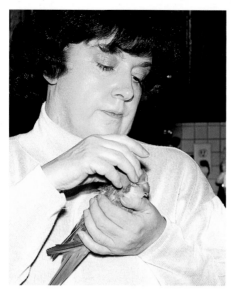

- Are you willing to have behavioral records transferred?
- Does this bird have a regular groomer, pet sitter, or other regular service providers? Name and describe:
- Does this bird have any physical or behavioral conditions that would affect its ability to reproduce, such as a physical imperfection, masturbation syndrome, egg eating, infertility, previous health compromises, etc.?
- Please list any additional conditions affecting this bird:

This history is true and complete to the best of my knowledge.

(Signature of Current/Former Owner/Address/Telephone)

Transfer of Ownership

If the Quaker parrot is going directly to the permanent new home, the only further document would transfer ownership from the current/former owner to the new owner. At least the following suggested elements should be included in a *Transfer of Ownership* form:

- Name of person(s) called "current/former owner":
- Name of person(s) called "new owner":
- Name of individual or organization supervising the adoption
- New owner agrees to assume all physical and financial responsibility for the bird:
- New owner understands that the bird is adopted in as-is condition and neither the current/former owner, the temporary care provider (where necessary) nor the individual or organization supervising the adoption is liable for any preexisting or developing physical, medical, or behavioral conditions affecting this bird or other birds in the household:
- New owner agrees that this bird shall not be sold at any time in the future, and that if lifestyle changes require that the bird find a new home, the individual or organization supervising this adoption will select and supervise the adoption:
- Date and time of transfer of ownership:
- This agreement should be signed by all participating parties.

The Foster Home

If no permanent home is available for the bird and it must be removed from the present home immediately, then temporary housing—a foster home—must be provided until an appropriate placement home can be found. This makes things much more complicated, since there is always a possibility of accident or illness or other misfortune in the temporary foster home.

Following are minimal suggested considerations for the *Temporary Care Agreement.*

- Name of bird:
- Name of temporary care provider:
- Name of individual or organization supervising the adoption (new owner):
- Name of person responsible for financial obligations for the bird while it is in temporary care:
- Temporary care provider agrees to quarantine the bird from all other birds for a period of at least one month.
- Temporary care provider shall not be held liable in the event of illness, injury, death, or other mishaps occurring during temporary care.
- Temporary care provider agrees that current/former owner and individual or organization supervising the adoption are not liable for illness, injury, death, or other mishaps occurring as a result of the temporary foster care.
- Conditions under which temporary foster care can be terminated by either the temporary care provider or by the individual or organization supervising the adoption:
- Date and time at which care of the bird is transferred to the temporary care provider:

Agreement should be signed by temporary care provider and the individual or organization supervising the adoption (new owner).

The Permanent Placement

Usually, the *Temporary Care Agreement* will terminate when a new permanent home is found. At that time, a *Transfer of Ownership* form can be provided to document the time and date of the new owner's responsibilities. Careful written records will prevent the vast majority of misunderstandings from occurring during adoption placements. I have never seen a serious misunderstanding relating to a well-documented adoption, and I have seen many serious and bitter misunderstandings that developed during unwritten, handshake adoptions.

This parrot's "body language" is obviously "happy."

Chapter Ten
Regulation, Retrieval, and Naturalization

In the City

Because of concerns that escaped Quaker parrots could become naturalized residents of the local environment, Quaker parrot ownership is restricted with banding or other regulations in several states. Breeding Quakers, their ownership, and even transportation is prohibited in some states. Ellen Krueger of the Quaker Parakeet Society reminded me that one state to ban these little guys is Pennsylvania, the Quaker state, founded by human Quakers.

Quaker parrots have been known to live wild in the United States since 1964.

Because laws and regulations change frequently in the United States, any published list of state regulations can be quickly out of date. Notably, Quaker parrot ownership is regulated in every state. A list of states where Quakers were banned, partially banned, or ownership is otherwise in question as of November 1996 appears on page 111.

It's extremely difficult to obtain reliable information about the current status of these laws and regulations. Callers are often given different opinions from different sources within the same department in the same state on the same day. Many individual birds are legal in their states as a result of being "grandfathered in," that is, the birds were already in their present homes when the regulation passed.

Restrictions, Escape, and Retrieval

Quaker parrots have been observed as residents of the eastern United States since 1964. The 1980 edition of *Peterson Field Guides to*

State	Law or Regulation
California	Illegal to own or sell
Connecticut	Illegal to own or sell (reportedly changing)
Georgia	Illegal to own or sell
Kansas	Illegal to own or sell (reportedly changing)
Kentucky	Illegal to own or sell
Hawaii	Illegal to own or sell
New Jersey	Illegal to own or sell
New York	Legal to own with registration and banding
Pennsylvania	Illegal to own or sell
Tennessee	Illegal to own or sell
Virginia	Legal to own with breeder or seller registration
Wyoming	Illegal to own or sell

Information Provided by Jeff Sofa/Quaker Home Page INTERNET:taz@usa.net

Eastern Birds reports that although the Quaker "...has attempted to nest in a number of states from Massachusetts to Florida and west to Oklahoma."*

This is an interesting development considering the birds' feared potential as pernicious agricultural pest and harasser and displacer of native birds. In the Quaker parrot's native Argentina, the bird is considered opportunistic. The bird's native range has advanced with the ever-increasing expansion of human cities. That is, unlike macaws, who have diminished as a result of habitat (nesting site) loss, the Quaker parrot has increased numbers as a result of predation on farmlands that have replaced wild habitat.

* Peterson, Roger Tory. *Peterson Field Guides to Eastern Birds,* Houghton Mifflin Company, 1980, page 178.

Some insight into the Quaker parrot's naturalization in the United States might be provided by David Wright, who has studied feral Quakers in Connecticut and on the eastern coast of the United States. Wright

Parrots add one more layer of diversity to North American cities.

Wild-caught Quakers readjust easily to life outdoors.

suggests that feral Quaker parrots survive in areas where there is year-round food, an abundance of large trees, and proximity to a large body of fresh water. He observes that Quakers do not leave the immediate area from which they were fledged, and therefore have not proliferated as feared in areas where they have become a fixture.

These birds aren't flying into our shrinking woodlands or countryside taking native habitat from North American wildlife. They aren't crowding out songbirds or woodpeckers or scissor-tailed flycatchers; they're competing with us! Bold little hook-billed invaders are living in our cities, coexisting side by side with humans, eating the fruits of our grasses and ornamental plants.

They aren't alone. Human-specific habitat is increasingly shared

Pale Male

During the winter of 1991, instead of merely migrating through as hundreds of hawks do every year, a red-tailed hawk established New York's Central Park as his territory. Called "Pale Male" for his light coloring, this exceptional bird has inspired a huge cadre of fans who carefully record his day-to-day existence in one of the world's most human-populous cities.

Every spring Pale Male and his mate go to nest on an angel-ornamented ledge over Fifth Avenue. The vision of birds of prey hunting in midtown Manhattan inspires millions of New Yorkers as well as others who travel from around the world to watch this incredible ongoing survival story.

While the food supply is plentiful, eating can be dangerous, for many pigeons are poisoned every day in the Big Apple. Poison the prey, poison the predator. Pale Male has survived several mates. He has survived being injured by an ever-present gang of crows and in ten years raised nineteen offspring. For some of the most beautiful bird photos you've ever seen, go to *http://www.palemale.com*.

by non-native birds, squirrels, opos-sums, coyotes, foxes, bats, and even reptiles, amphibians, and fish. We seldom hear complaints about environmental damage caused by dogs, cats, horses, or livestock. These species are so dear that most of us can't imagine life without them, but their presence does affect the environment. Additionally, methane produced by contented cattle, goats, and pigs fattening themselves up for an ever-increasing number of human dinner tables is said to be changing the air we breathe, the entire planet's atmosphere. Methane gas is second only to carbon dioxide in terms of contribution to global warming. Atmospheric methane levels have doubled in the last 200 years.*

I have watched free-flying Quaker "pairs" make loosely woven temporary nests in Colorado. Even though some of these birds have long survived outdoors, they apparently have not produced offspring.

I have not yet seen a hand-fed domestic bird with the necessary skills to survive outdoors. Even the attempted reintroduction of domestic thick-billed parrots specially trained to live wild has demonstrated that most domestically raised parrots probably have little or no chance of surviving wild. In my experience, when hand-fed Quakers accidentally fly away, they usually wind up going to a human rather than seeking outdoor food and water sources.

From many years of recapturing feral Quakers in Colorado, I believe that most of the birds living wild in this country are escaped, wild-caught, imported birds or their descendents.

---

* http://education.arm.gov/methane.html

Chapter Eleven
Quakers in Aviculture and in Real Life

Many people who breed Quaker parrots focus solely on producing "normal" chicks. It's simple. It's part of what has always been attractive about Quaker breeding. There is no need to worry about selective breeding for color, but colors occur naturally as a result of pair bonds formed by individual members of the group. Sometimes spontaneous color mutations occur, but Quaker parrots are increasingly bred for color.

That is not to say that all Quakers look alike, though most do. Some Quakers have larger eyes than others. Some have pink feet, others have gray or black feet, but we don't really know whether this is an individual characteristic or a matter of subspecies. There's so little difference between subspecies in aviculture, that even the birds don't appear to notice.

Color Mutations

The development of color mutations in Quaker parrots is one of the most exciting developments in aviculture today. Color mutations may begin accidentally or spontaneously. An aviculturist might unknowingly purchase a bird that is related to the intended mate, doubling up a recessive color gene invisible in either bird. Thus, a new color is born.* Further breeding of birds known to carry this color, whether visible or not, establishes that mutation in the species.

Rather than introducing color into a species of bird, mutation is actually an inherited trait causing an inability or partial inability to produce one color or another. For example, the colors yellow and blue combine to produce green. In the Quaker parrot, the bird's physiology must generate yellow and blue to make them green. When blue, the first color mutation in monks appeared in the 1980s, it was produced when a bird inherited a genetic trait that caused an inability to produce yellow in its feathers. Much later, a mutation appeared eliminating the ability to produce blue in feathers and the yellow mutation was born. While color mutations

*Jordan, Rick, Correspondence, April 2004.

in some species may be small individuals, some of the largest Quakers I have ever seen were lutinos.

Cinnamon Quakers inherit a trait causing normally dark pigments to appear lighter. Some birds produce more black while others may produce almost none. A Quaker parrot inheriting a cinnamon gene that blocks a great deal of dark pigment appears very light yellow with very little blue making very little green. Even the beak, feet, and eyes may be lighter. Albinoism is the inherited trait causing the inability to produce all colors. True albinos lack pigmentation even in the eyes, giving the characteristic "red" eyes showing the color of the retina.

Closing Thoughts:
Mr. Herbie's Story

"This is Kawanita," the voice on the other end of the phone line would say. "Have you found Mr. Herbie yet?" Every day the same voice asked the same question. By the time I left the Katrina 911 parrot alert rescue operation, I'd heard it a dozen times.

About a week after returning home, I received an e-mail.

"I'm looking for my parrot...," the message began.

Kawanita was still trying to find Mr. Herbie! She'd spent hours, days, weeks on the phone, on foot, and on the Internet and was still hoping to find her bird, still hoping to discover more resources for locating Mr. Herbie. She knew he had survived Hurricane Katrina. He had survived

the floods. Did he survive the evacuation?

I'll try to tell the story just the way she told me.

They met at a pet store in New Orleans where Mr. Herbie had a reputation for biting the hands of those interested in buying him. He wound up living with Kawanita, Soldier (an adopted 18-month-old Rottweiler), and two jenday conures; and they were all home the day the nearby levee gave way. Grabbing the Quaker parrot first, Kawanita managed to get Mr. Herbie up to the highest point in the kitchen, but the waters rose quickly. Before she could likewise situate the jendays, her house was swamped, the conures were lost, and she and Soldier wound up swimming for their lives.

A Stick in TIme: Nesting Provisions

In the 1980s, I interviewed Denver aviculturist, Ilsa Goshorn, about her Quaker colony breeding practices. Every January, Ilse would cut the backs off of eight Christmas trees and then wire two trees into opposite sides of each corner high up of a giant flight cage. The flat back of each tree fit against the cage wall and branches interlocked with the tree wired to the other side of the corner. Building materials in the form of sticks cut off the back of those trees were provided on shelves. The birds began constructing new nests where the branches of the trees interlocked at the corners of their enclosure.

This was the first I had heard about stick-stealing behaviors in Quaker colonies. Ilsa reported that a continuous supply of sticks had to be provided or the birds would steal them from each others' nests. In fact, she had to pick up fallen sticks, run them through the dishwasher, and put them back on the shelves, as the birds preferred to steal sticks already in a nest rather than pick up sticks from the floor.

I supposed this stick-stealing behavior was a captive adaptation. Until I watched wild monks in Ft. Lauderdale with Jon-Mark Davet, I had no idea this was natural wild behavior. No matter how many hundreds of sticks are on the ground, monks constantly steal them from each others' nests. At least once each season Ilse said she had to pick up fallen babies from the floor when neighbors had stolen enough sticks to collapse a nest. Indeed, when researching this book, I learned that the most common cause of death in wild Quakers—whether from lightning or wind or rain or larcenous neighbor—is nest collapse.

Kawanita soon became exhausted in the swift current, barely managing to keep her head above water, trying to cling to her house. As she struggled, Soldier worked his way to her, pushed her, paddling forcefully. He pinned her against the outside wall of her home. With his help, she managed to stay afloat until the water reached the lower edge of the roof. He stayed with her, stabilizing her, so she could climb onto the roof. But the roof was too steep for Soldier to climb. When he began to tire, Soldier swam to the next-door neighbor's carport and struggled to safety. They waited overnight on separate, adjacent rooftops. By morning, the current had slowed. Kawanita braved the black water to swim over to join Soldier. There they waited together, again.

They were there for quite some time with nothing to drink and everything was very quiet, but Kawanita thought she could hear wild bird sounds. How could that be? She didn't see any birds? Was she hallucinating?

As the bird sounds were repeated, they became more and more familiar.

They had a distinct Quaker parrot accent.

"Soldier. Soldier. Comm'ere Soldier."

Mr. Herbie's voice!

"Soldier. Soldier. Comm'ere Soldier."

Even though the house had been submerged in water to the roofline, somehow, Mr. Herbie had survived! He was inside the house!

Again braving the waters, Kawanita found Mr. Herbie in an air space formed against the kitchen ceiling. She managed to carry him from her house to the neighbor's carport rooftop in a Tupperware container with holes punched in it. The three of them waited there until a neighbor came in a boat and took them to her house a few blocks away.

This neighbor's house had no roof, but it had walls. It seemed safe until another levee breech. Kawanita and her neighbor were forced to leave with an official evacuation team. Mr. Herbie and Soldier were not allowed to go with them.

Surely it's easy to understand why she couldn't take a Rottweiler. But why couldn't she take a Tupperware container with a Quaker parrot inside?

When I spoke with Kawanita the week of September 25th, she'd

Regulation changes since Hurricane Katrina allow a pet bird to be evacuated more easily.

located Soldier in a foster home in another state. As far as I know, Mr. Herbie has not been found. I don't know about Kawanita, but I've never given up hope. Because I've seen so many lost bird stories resolve favorably even years later, I still dream that Mr. Herbie's somewhere down there in Louisiana, maybe living in a tree making baby Quakers and telling them stories about Sailor and Kawanita.

Glossary

Please note that the following definitions set forth the meanings of these words as they are used specifically in this text. They are not intended to be full and complete definitions.

aggression: hostile nipping, biting, or chasing.

ailanthus: trees of heaven, weed tree common in older urban cities in the United States. So named for a Moluccan word meaning, "tree that grows up to the sky." Soft, easy to grip branches well-suited to Quaker parrot perches.

allofeeding: mutual feeding or simulated mutual feeding. One of several behaviors related to breeding.

allopreening: mutual preening or simulated mutual preening, for example, a human scratching a parrot's neck.

anthropomorphizing: ascribing human attributes to a non-human thing.

baby days: a young parrot's first, impressionable weeks in the new home, an idyllic period before the baby bird's instincts for independence, dominance, and exploration develop. *See also:* honeymoon period.

band: coded metal device placed around a bird's leg for identification purposes.

behavioral environment: behavioral conditions, especially redundant or habitual behaviors, present in the bird and in individuals around the bird.

bite: use of the parrot's beak in a manner intended to cause damage or injury.

bite zone: area in front of the bird's beak in which the hand can easily be bitten but not easily stepped on (described on pages 18–19).

blood feather: unopened immature feather which is completely or partially covered by a bluish/white membrane indicating that the feather is currently supplied with blood.

bonding: the connection with another bird, a human, object, or location which a bird exhibits and defends.

breeding-related behaviors: behaviors with a source related to breeding habits in the wild such as arranging, (nest-building), allopreening, allofeeding, masturbating, copulating, and aggression at the nest site (cage).

cavity-breeding: describes breeding-related chewing behaviors of parrots other than Quaker parrots.

chasing: to drive away by pursuing.

command: an order or instruction given by a dominant individual.

covert: a layer of covering feathers as in the gray and green feathers covering the bird's down.

developmental period: a behavioral period wherein the bird's instincts for dominance, independence, and aggression are first manifest. *See also:* terrible twos.

dominance: control, enforcing individual will over others.

down: the small fuzzy feathers next to the body that are normally covered by coverts.

drama: any activity that brings an excited response either positive or negative.

earthquake: a behavioral correction performed during step-up practice. *See also:* Wobble Distraction (page 21).

emargination: notching on flight feathers facilitating maneuverability in flight.

eye contact: the act of maintaining eye-to-eye gaze.

flock/flock mates: as it applies to a companion bird, human companions sharing a home with a captive parrot.

forage: the search for food.

gathering: the process of hoarding food for future use.

good hand/bad hand: a behavioral technique designed to distract a bird from biting.

grooming: the process of having the companion parrot's wing feathers trimmed, nails cut or filed, and, if necessary, beak shaped.

habit: redundant behavior that has become a fixed part of the bird's conduct.

hand-fed: a parrot that as a neonate was fed by humans rather than birds

handling techniques: methods used by humans to stimulate and maintain successful tactile interactions with companion parrots.

harvesting: removing ripe fruits or vegetables so that they may provide future forage. *See also:* gathering.

honeymoon period: a young parrot's first, impressionable weeks in the new home, an idyllic period before the bird's instinct for dominance and exploration develop. *See also:* baby days.

independence: improvising and enjoying self-rewarding behaviors.

juvenile: immature behaviors unrelated to nesting or breeding.

language: a method of verbal communication wherein multiple individuals use the same sounds or groups of sounds to convey the same meanings.

mandible: the beak, horny protuberance with which the bird bites.

manzanita: commercially available hardwood branches, that in small sizes are suitable for Quaker parrot perches.

mate: the individual to whom a Quaker parrot is primarily bonded.

model: a learning process by which one individual copies behavior from another individual.

molt: the cyclical shedding and replacing of feathers.

neonate: a baby parrot that cannot yet eat food independently.

nest/nesting: the act of constructing a structure for the purpose of reproduction.

nest box: a human constructed box for bird nesting.

nipping: an accidental, unintentional, or non-aggressive bite not intended to cause damage.

parakeet: a parrot with a long, graduated tail.

parrot: a bird with a notched upper mandible, a mallet shaped tongue, and four toes (two facing front and two facing back).

patterning: stimulating an individual to repeat behaviors through the process of repeatedly drilling the behavior.

polymer fume fever: the condition that can kill a bird that is exposed to fumes from Teflon heated to 500°F.

preen: to groom the feathers, as with "combing" and "zipping" them with the beak.

prompt: a cue, here used for the physical cue to cause the bird to step up.

psittacine: any parrot.

quaking: palsy-like feeding response of baby quakers that may be occasionally repeated in compromised or courting adults.

quarantine: enforced isolation for the prevention of disease transmission.

recapture: to apprehend or recover possession of a parrot that has flown away.

regurgitate: voluntary or involuntary production of partially digested food from the crop. *See also:* allofeeding.

reinforce: process of rewarding a behavior that we wish to become habitual.

rescue: fortuitous removal from frightening circumstances.

rival: a competitor, one who competes for reinforcement or reward.

roaming: unsupervised explorations away from approved cage or play areas.

roost: the place where a bird usually sleeps.

self-rewarding behavior: an activity that is enacted solely for the pleasure of doing it.

sexual behavior: self-rewarding breeding-related behavior.

sexual maturity: the period during which breeding-related behaviors become prominent in the bird's overall behavior.

signaling: anything that warns, alerts, or telegraphs an intention or apparent intention which might generate a reaction.

status: positioning related to dominance within the pecking order.

step-up: practice of giving the step-up command with the expectation that the bird will perform the behavior.

stress: any stimulus, especially fear or pain, that inhibits normal psychological, physical, or behavioral balance.

subspecies: a subdivision of species, especially by color or geographical characteristics.

substrata: material placed in the bottom of the bird's cage or play area to contain mess and droppings.

sumac: a small, sparsely branching weed tree found in pastures and adjoining land throughout most of the United States. Sumac is not poisonous, but rather is a common food source for many native species of birds. It is suitable for use as Quaker parrot perches and toys.

terrible twos: a behavioral period wherein the bird's instincts for dominance, independence, and aggression are first manifest. *See also:* developmental period.

tool: an implement that is manipulated to accomplish a particular function.

toxin: any substance that causes illness or death through exposure to it.

toy: any tool for producing self-rewarding behavior.

trap: a device used to recapture a free-flying bird.

vocabulary: words or elements comprising a language.

window of opportunity: a finite period during which something can be accomplished, a period of time during which behavior can be changed.

wobble distraction: a behavioral correction performed during step-up practice (see page 21). *See also:* earthquake.

Useful Addresses and Literature

Books

Athan, *Guide to a Well-Behaved Parrot*, Barron's Educational Series, Inc., Hauppauge, NY, 2007.

Athan, *Parrots, a Complete Pet Owner's Manual*, Barron's Educational Series, Inc., Hauppauge, NY, 2002.

Athan, Deter, *The Second-hand Parrot*, Barron's Educational Series, Inc., Hauppauge, NY, 2002.

Burgmann, *Feeding Your Pet Bird*, Barron's Educational Series, Inc., Hauppauge, NY, 1993.

Davie, Davie and Athan; *Parrots in the City, One Bird's Struggle for a Place on the Planet*, The Quaker Parakeet Society, Eugene, OR, 2004.

Krueger, *The Fonzie Chronicles*, A Way With Words, Action, Massachusetts, 2006.

Resources
a-waywithwords.net

Bird Talk and Birds USA
P.O. Box 6050
Mission Viejo, CA 92690

BrooklynParrots.com

Goodfeather.com

parrotsinthecity.com

positivelyparrots.com

Quaker Parakeet Society
P.O. Box 7241
Eugene, OR 97401

qp-society.com/

Quakerville.com

Index